Un Trip through the Mind Jail
y Otras Excursions

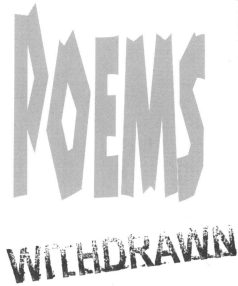

Also by raúlrsalinas

East of the Freeway: Reflections de Mi Pueblo

Un Trip through the Mind Jail y Otras Excursions

POEMS

raúlrsalinas

Arte Público Press
Houston, Texas
1999

This volume is made possible through grants from the National Endowment for the Arts (a federal agency), the Lila Wallace-Reader's Digest Fund and the City of Houston through The Cultural Arts Council of Houston, Harris County.

Recovering the past, creating the future

Arte Público Press
University of Houston
Houston, Texas 77204-2174

Cover art by Juan F. Bazan
Cover design by James F. Brisson
Interior line art by José Montoya

Raúlrsalinas.
    Un trip through the mind jail / by raúlrsalinas.
    p.   cm.
    ISBN 1-55885-275-1
    1. Mexican American Poetry. 2. Mexican American prisoners
Poetry. 3. Prisons Poetry. I. Title.
PS3568.A82T75   1999
811'.54--dc21   99-34719
                                       CIP

♾ The paper used in this publication meets the requirements of the American National Standard for Information Sciences—Permanence of Paper for Printed Library Materials, ANSI Z39.48-1984.

9 0 1 2 3 4 5 6 7 8   10 9 8 7 6 5 4 3 2 1

Contents

Preface

Some Reflections on Twenty Years of
Un Trip through the Mind Jail y Otras Excursions

Louis Mendoza

With this long-overdue republication of *Un Trip Through the Mind Jail y Otras Excursions,* Arte Público Press continues its tradition of maintaining the legacy of Latino letters by keeping important works available to the public. Long considered a classic of Chicano poetry, this collection is one of many significant works to emerge from independent Latino presses. Originally published in 1980 by San Francisco-based Editorial Pocho-Che, *Trip* quickly sold out its press run of 2,000. Its status as a collector's item is perhaps best exemplified by the fact that the book cannot be found, no matter how meticulously one searches, in a used bookstore. Quite simply it was then, and is now, a work that strikes readers as a book they should keep as a cherished component of their personal collections.

Several poems in this collection, from the classic paean to the barrio "A Trip through the Mind Jail" (the author's signature poem), to "Los Caudillos," "Ciego/Sordo/Mudo," "Homenaje al Pachuco," "Crash Landing," "News from San Quentin," and "Muse Moving Mountain," to name but a few, have been widely anthologized in collections of American, Chicano, Latino, and political poetry. The enduring nature of Salinas's poetry speaks to the continuing relevance of this poet's vision as a voice of resistance and a bard of the streets. By not having access to this entire collection, until now, many readers have been denied the fuller context and range of this poet's work, which provides a rich intertextuality and a wider variety of subject matter for comprehending Salinas's aesthetics.

Many critics, scholars, and students of Salinas's poetry struggle to interpret his work because it is not easily classified into a single school of style or thought. Though he is most often identified as a Chicano Movement poet for the highly stylized, politically charged expressions of social protest that shape his work, many commentators on Salinas miss his both subtle and profound engagement and subsequent revision of U. S. and Latin American literary traditions. There are those critics, to be sure, who have misread the context and style of his work, just as there are those who see his range of styles as either undisciplined or eclectic. And, indeed there may be some truth to those judgments, but there is also more depth to his work that we can expect a newer generation of readers to discover as they take advantage of the re-publication of *Trip* to make their own evaluation of Salinas's literary and political significance.

If recognition and material gain define success, Salinas is only half-successful. In Chicano literary studies he is seen as both a foundational figure of *pinto* poetry and the Chicano Renaissance, though his reputation may suffer these days from the limited availability of his work. As is true for many worthy writers, Salinas has not been a commercial success. In terms that are often misused, Salinas is a genuine organic intellectual of his community, one who struggles to articulate and realize a new social order. Tomas Ybarra-Frausto's original introduction, included here, remains one of the most definitive statements of Salinas's poetics. Situating the different stages of the poems represented in this collection in terms of the defining experience of incarceration, Ybarra-Frausto accurately identifies the multiple literary and life influences on Salinas. Ybarra-Frausto's claim that Salinas's poetry is simultaneously resistant, therapeutic, autobiographical, and transformative work that "might be typical and representative of the Chicano community" is astute and can be seen as true of all Salinas's poetry, including his most recent collection, *East of the Freeway: Reflections de mi Pueblo* and in his forthcoming *Indio Trails: A Xicano Odyssey thru Indian Country*.

What Ybarra-Frausto could not have seen as this collection was just making its way into the world was the many rebirths and artistic transformations of the title poem. Very few poems touch people across time, space, and cultures in the way this poem has. The many multi-media adaptations of *Un Trip Through the Mind Jail*, from stage to film to opera, are powerful testimony to the poet's ability to render a culturally specific sense of place that is at once an excruciatingly honest and unromanticized examination of both the intimate and intimidating dynamics of barrio culture, even as it is expressed in universal terms.

As Salinas's poems from his "captive years" and his "poems of partial freedom" are read at the dawn of the new century, the twenty- to forty-year contrast in social context bears mention. Salinas first received recognition for his work as a writer who "comprehends that as a Chicano *pinto* (convict), he [could] serve as a representative and spokesman against the repressive reality of America within and outside the prison walls" (Ybarra-Frausto Introduction, page 7). Emerging in a period of heightened social consciousness about the unjust and disproportionate imprisonment of people of color in this country, a period marked by clandestine government repression against civil rights activists, Salinas's work was always already situated in the context of the Prisoners' Rights Movement (known as the Prison Rebellion Years to those inside), alongside the work of Ricardo Sánchez, Luis Talamantez, Jimmy Santiago Baca, Judy Lucero, Etheridge Knight, George Jackson, and Eldridge Cleaver, among others. In fact, the title poem was originally dedicated to Eldridge Cleaver, a dedication that Salinas withdrew when Cleaver's own political commitments changed. Today, with a few exceptions, there is very little public attention given to the ever increasing and ever expanding Prison Industrial Complex as a larger and larger proportion of our population, most of whom are very young, and are incarcerated for longer periods of time with little regard for rehabilitation. They are victims of a judicial system hell-bent on addressing the symptoms of a society gone awry and not the underlying causes that drive people to live outside the law. Though we may not hear the voices of the hundreds of thousands of imprisoned social prisoners in our country, we can bet that they are indeed undergoing transformation and giving voice to it through art. As readers follow the poet's journey from transgression to transformation in this collection, they would do well to remember the representative dimension of Salinas's voice of experience even when it juxtaposes with their own.

Salinas's primary motif in this collection, one that is also present in his other works, is that of the journey. This is no ordinary literary sojourn, for it is not one marked merely by travel or landscapes, though history and social geography play an important role. Nor is Salinas's journey a philosophical quest for enlightenment, though indeed he documents a spiritual and intellectual period of growth even as he critiques bourgeois notions of knowledge and individual freedom. Rather, the journey is linked to social movements that are occurring inside and outside of the walls of prison, and this is the context for the poet's transformation from individual alienation to rage and finally resistance. In the process he claims a place in the world as an artist, an intellectual, and political philosopher consumed with the idea that justice inside and outside of prisons is a realizable vision. It is a quest he continues pursuing today, one that can be seen in his work with the Leonard Peltier Defense Committee, the Free Mumia Campaign, the Comité en Solidaridad con Chiapas y Mexico, and his own local project, Save Our Youth (SOY).

Salinas's poems document a life shaped by hostile social institutions. But his ultimate emergence as a poet activist did not result from the socialization and reform policies of school and prisons; instead this occurred *in spite of* oppressive institutions that sought to stifle his creativity and independence. Norman Mailer, in his introduction to Jack Henry Abbott's *In the Belly of the Beast* (New York: Vintage Books, 1981, page xii) makes a point applicable to Salinas's situation:

> There is a paradox at the core of penology, and from it derives the thousand ills and afflictions of the prison system. It is not that only the worst of the young are sent to prison, but the best—that is, the proudest, the bravest, the most daring, the most enterprising, and the most undefeated of the poor. There starts the horror.

Salinas would never claim status as a poster child of prison reform—though he contributed to it in a period when it was sorely needed (as it is needed now). And though he was part of an imprisoned community of self-taught, highly disciplined radicals who seized control of their intellectual and political destiny, he will not laud prison for its reformatory possibilities. He knows too well that the prison system is designed to bring out the worst prejudices and most brutally abusive acts of power in people—guards and convicts alike. What we can learn from this collection, as we can learn from many other prison artists, is that just as the harsh reality of prisons can serve as a microcosm for the larger world, it is also true that his insights and epiphanies are relevant to all of us . . . if we but listen.

Salinas is the consummate writer, constantly putting pen to paper since he discovered his literary voice. To our detriment he is not a strong advocate of his own work, rarely sending his work out for review and publication. To our benefit, however, he saves his work. In 1994, under the urging of Ben Olguín, then a graduate student at Stanford University, Roberto Trujillo, the collector and archivist for Stanford's impressive Mexican American Special Collection, successfully sought and acquired Salinas's personal archives. This important acquisition contains over twenty linear feet of unpublished creative prose and poetry, correspondence, and other materials that document Salinas's prolific literary productions and his longtime involvement with social justice work.

Salinas's self-introduction to *Trip* in "Hey! World!!!" is composed of excerpts from his prison letters, which are now part of the Salinas collection at Stanford. This epistolary montage can provide a template for readers to understand not only the conditions of Salinas's incarceration, but the multivocalic, multilingual style that characterize his struggle against systematic dehumanization. It is a struggle to retain his intellectual and psychological integrity that can also be found in the structure, rhythm, and content of his poetry. What we are offered here finally is an opportunity to expand the boundaries of our own lives by being invited to enter into the heart and soul of a man who seeks what we all do, the freedom to define the terms of our lives, of our very humanity.

Introduction to the First Edition

The poetry of Raúl Salinas is an impressive and important contribution to Chicano literature. Mainly written in various prisons over a span of fifteen years, Salinas's collected verse is shaped by two primary experiences–his victimization by society at large and his long experience with incarceration. The prison experience of nearly two decades serves as a mediator between Salinas as victim and artist. Imprisonment defines the sensibility and establishes the formal and thematic elements which are elaborated in most of his poetry. The long, bitter years spent behind steel bars, within the mountains of brick, served to activate his poetic imagination towards an incessant focus on the themes of memory and reminiscence, oppression and imminent apocalypse, and ultimately songs of partial freedom and liberation.

Salinas's poetics and his political maturation, both evolving since his entry into prison in 1957, coalesce during the social catclysms of the sixties. During his lonely encapsulation in juvenile detention centers, jails, and prisons, Raúl Salinas does not suffer from alienation from the Chicano community. Instead, his bondage leads to reflection, analysis, and recognition of how his personal loss of freedom parallels the condition of oppression suffered by the Chicanos within the American society. He further comprehends that as a Chicano *pinto* (convict), he can serve as a representative and spokesman against the repressive reality of America within and outside the prison walls.

Choosing to focus on a social reality manifestly at odds with the dominant culture, his poetry, like the work of most contemporary Chicano writers, has not been readily accepted into mainstream

7

American literature. Nevertheless, the poetic production of Raúl Salinas spanning nearly two decades presents a coherent, moving, and powerful interpretation of the Chicano experience.

The poems in this collection are arranged chronologically and establish both the literary and political maturation of the artist. In presenting poems from Salinas's early, middle, and recent periods, we can see three continual preoccupations:

(1) the relationship of poetry to social experience,
(2) the manipulation of the autobiographical mode as a means toward integration of the poetic self,
(3) the evolution of a thematic axis that revolves around images of a voyage, a trip, or a journey.

EARLY PRISON POEMS:
SOLEDAD TO HUNTSVILLE, 1958-1964

Like that of most writers, the early poetry of Raúl Salinas initiates a search for an authentic voice and a personal style. Although experimental and uneven, poems from this initial period are open and explicit, sharing a sense of discovery and excitement that is direct and unabashed. Already they indicate how the interior human psyche dominates his imagination. Many of these initial poems serve as a constant revision of the self charting a spiritual quest that will be later joined to the key metaphor of a journey or trip through which the poet will expand the boundaries of experience in pursuit of an integrated sense of being.

During this period of apprenticeship, Salinas incorporates into his poetry influences from two distinctly American sources: the music of jazz and the literature of the Beats. Finding close affinities with Allen Ginsberg, Gregory Corso, and Jack Kerouac, Salinas is attracted by both their stance and their aesthetic. Poems such as "Jazz: A Nascence," "Epiphany," "Did Charlie Have a Horn," and especially "Lamento" have a free form improvised quality akin to musical riffs. They recall Kerouac's notions in "Essentials of Spontaneous Prose" comparing the writer to a jazz saxophonist in search of language as an undisturbed flow from the mind. Other fundamentals of beat poetry that influence the evolution of Salinas's style include a sense of romantic nihilism, exaltation of the emotional dimension of experience, and above all an insistent and voluble celebration of the self. These early poems represent for Salinas a period of gestation and serious dedication to writing.

THE FORGING OF A POETICS:
LEAVENWORTH TO MARION, 1967-1972

This middle period remains a fruitful and important stage in Salinas's poetic development. Apart from jazz and the black idiom, three other sources: the Chicano movement, the mobilization of prisoners "inside the walls," and national and international political movement serve as fundamental nutrients to his poetic imagination. Although confined behind bars, Salinas maintains extensive correspondence with individuals and groups involved in the same tumultuous political activities of the era. Analysis of information documenting these black, Puerto Rican, and Chicano liberation struggles help to politicize him inside the joint in much the same way that actual participation in the struggles changes the consciousness of those outside the walls. During this time span, which encompasses the murder of several hundred students at Tlatelolco (Mexico), the Cuban Revolution, and the prison rebellions at San Quentin and Attica, Salinas records his psychic transformation:

. . . un proceso de transformación mental; see it occurring, feel it surging within, it's at once, amazing, extremely difficult to grasp, painful and frightening!!!

An end result of this self-actualization was the gaining of a firm identity as a convict/artist. Additionally, Salinas recognizes that his imprisonment should not deter his becoming a representative voice of the Chicano collectively, both being victims of the same societal racism and oppression. The publication of poems such as "Ciego, Sordo, Mudo" and "Los Caudillos" responds to the dynamics of the Chicano Movement in its evolution up to that time. As the momentum of Chicano insurgency mounted, Salinas's generation in their diverse voices, which included José Montoya, Abelardo Delgado, Ricardo Sánchez, and Tigre, called for a retrieval of the strengths within their cultural tradition. For Salinas, this recapturing of his heritage signals a shift toward an inward focus in his poetics. The elusive mysteries of his own identity enmeshed within forgotten events and relationships with individuals out of his past become recurrent themes. Separate poems are but fragments of one prolonged sequence of autobiography. Each remains beautifully focused on the vital facts of experience, especially the experience of growing up in a barrio. The use of the autobiographical mode demonstrates how the convict/poet utilizes personal experiences as a reflection of the message and the motives for its communication. Exploration of the self is not intended as a display of individuality but an attempt at showing how the author's experience might be typical and representative of the Chicano community. The most significant sample of this poetic autobiography is Salinas's first major poem, "A Trip through the Mind Jail." Here the poet creates a transmutation of life in the barrio into a landscape of the imagination that is universal and particular at the same time. "A Trip through the Mind Jail" is a psychological portrait and journey into the self. Incarcerated in a tiny cell at the United States Federal Penitentiary in Leavenworth, Kansas, Salinas allows the dual agents of memory and imagination to embark on a labyrinthine voyage seeking to encounter the pure center of meaning in his life. "A Trip through the Mind Jail" is undoubtedly a breakthrough poem for Raúl Salinas. In it he consolidates one of his persistent, almost obsessive themes–the trip or journey in search of spiritual integration and completion.

POEMS OF (PARTIAL) FREEDOM:
SEATTLE AND BEYOND, 1971-1979

Upon his release from Marion Federal Prison in Illinois, on November 27, 1972, Raúl Salinas arrives in Seattle and accepts admission to an academic program at the University of Washington. This venture to the Northwest has had a lasting effect on his psyche as well as his poetry. Responses to societal wounds and past experiences as a convict still inform his writing but the natural landscape of his new home and especially contact with Northwest Indian people has provided new vistas and themes.

Whereas previously Salinas developed a perspective from the jail outwards to the community, now the viewpoint will be from the community back to the prison. An obsessive question is the meaning of freedom. Facing the oppression and stark realities of life "on the outside," the poet comprehends that its liberty is a sham ("es puro pedo"). Seeking to internalize this ironic fact, Salinas uses his past convict experience to reflect on his present illusory independence. In these early Seattle poems, recurrent images of closure and encapsulation such as "jaulas horrorosas," "mausoleums of lore," "mi celda solitaria," "dungeons built by evil men," and "obscures corredores" project a hallucenogenic inhuman landscape that becomes "la cárcel de terror" from which the poet as a forlorn refugee seeks escape. He remains trapped by a futile present and excruciating past.

If the past experience of incarceration remains a permanent source of inspiration, the poet's new environment assumes a powerful impact. The trauma of adjusting to a new lifestyle is mitigated only by the natural beauty of the Pacific Northwest. Mount Rainier in all its awesome and majestic splendor becomes an important new image, its powers assiduously recorded in a poem series "Muse-Moving Mountain." More than any new acquaintance, the mountain is personified in different poems as coquette, a wise teacher, and a symbol of resistance and indifference to petty human travails. Aside from the mountain, the atmospheric essence of Seattle waterways, constant drizzle, and rain evokes a "soaking loneliness" with the prevalent moods being those of solitude and suffering.

The early seventies become years of constant movement for Salinas and a small band of stalwart Chicano activists from El Centro de La Raza in Seattle. He travels throughout the country to demonstrate solidarity with Puerto Rican nationalists, joins Indian fishing rights confrontations with the government, supports black mobilization (in the Northwest), and actively participates in Chicano demonstrations throughout the Southwest. As a consequence, Salinas's poetry moves from a painfully sensitive interior vision of the self outward towards an increasingly social vision.

By the mid-1970s, Salinas has shifted his political activity to focus on the development of Indian-Chicano Unity. Still based at El Centro de La Raza in Seattle, he criss-crosses the country several times over while on parole to participate in various Indian struggles such as support work for Wounded Knee, the Trail of Self-Determnination from Seattle to D.C. in 1976, the Hoopa Nation fishing standoff, the Puyallup/Nisqually encampments, the Cascadia Hospital takeover, and points in between. Moving beyond the dictums of the Chicano Movement of the mid-1960s, which sought philosophical relationships with indigenous cultures of the past, many Chicanos now seek alignment with the *contemporary* American Indian Movement, based on common concerns of areas of struggle.

A fundamental element of this indigenous world view is its spirituality, so that the American Indian Movement is seen not only as an advocate for Indian people but also as a spiritual rebirth of their nation. This coexistence of reflection and action seeps into the consciousness of Raúl Salinas and signals a central shift in his poetry, particularly towards the acquisition of a more collective voice.

The rhetorical urgency of previous collections is subdued by a breakthrough to quietness and serenity. Chants, prayers, and songs celebrate nature and sing of ancient powers of resistance. Immersed in living and studying the natural way of life, the poet finds new strength in ceremonies, lore, and belief systems of indigenous people from the "tundra main to the midwestern plains."

Nature is the root source of this ancient power and much of the Indian-inspired poetry of Salinas, written in the early 1970s, seems an effort at reconstituting the wonders and strength of the natural world, as if it were continually in danger of being lost. Spare, lean poems present simple pictorial images rooted in landscape and natural settings. Peaceful serenity seems the dominant mood, yet the poems constantly evoke Indian struggles for fishing rights, for ecological survival, and for cultural maintenance.

A central image present in many of the poems is the contrast between the traditional Indian way of life and the onslaught of White Man's technology.

Visiting Cuba in 1975 and 1977, Salinas encounters a society where culture and social action are joined. This strengthens his conviction of the link between art and poltics. Working in construction at the Campamento Julio Antonio Mella in the province of Guayabal, with periodic visits to La Habana, he has ample time to interact with "aficionados en el campo," as well as with intellectuals at La Unión de Escritores y Artistas Cubanos and the Ministry of Culture. Salinas is particularly inspired by a slim volume of poems, *Cuadernos Paralelos*, by Roberto Fernández Retamar. Upon his return to the Northwest, and following Retamar's example, Salinas compiles *Simplemente, Cuadernos Cubanos,* a compilation of short narrative poems which serve as a Cuban chronicle in which he records impressions and memories of his journey. Rather than documenting the revolution in terms of social achievement, Salinas focuses on the theme of childhood as a metaphor for the new society.

By now, a steady and progressive line of development in the poetry of Raúl Salinas from 1968 to the present can be charted. Its two dominant modes might be labled "diagnostic" and "therapeutic." In Salinas's continual advocacy of struggle as a way of life, he has employed his writing to expose and diagnose the ailments of American society with great fervor and intensity. An eloquent array of poems such as "In Memoriam: Riche," "Ciego/Sordo/Mudo," "Canción de la Bahía," and "A Trip through the Mind Jail," strive to articulate the truth of individuals living as members of marginalized sectors of American society. This poetry of social comment is at once a call to unity and battle. Written mainly in a direct exclamatory style of raw intensity, the poems in this modality can be brusque and inelegant but always they are alive, sustaining a strong presence of feeling.

The therapeutic modality is found primarily in the autobiographical poem sequences, in which Salinas utilizes fragments of autobiography to transcribe and fictionalize the accomplishments, disasters, and obessessive themes of his life. In poems such as "Pueblo Querido," "Journey II," "Canto (Just for the Hell of It)," "Crash Landing," and "Homenaje al Pachuco," the poet takes dictation from lived experience, transcribing the selected event into productive fiction. Confronting the deep, dark inwardness of his being, the literal self, placed at the center of the poem, meditates on its nature and meaning.

In this sense, Salinas's autobigraphical poetry is therapeutic, for as he examines and gives a verdict on himself and his life, the reader is being asked to respond with his or her own review and testimony.

The lively idiom of Salinas's total production registers some of the following characteristics: The form is fluid and improvisatory, presenting images as they flash through the mindscape, capturing the flux of his experience. His lines have a tough muscularity often charged with emotional or didactic content. A prose base gives the poems a momentum, a force that is well suited to poetry that ceases to focus on contemplation and representation, attempting to become an intervention in reality.

Opposed to a dry, ironic, dispassionately distant voice, Salinas speaks in an impassioned rhapsodic tone. His language is direct and explicitly discursive with strong injections of popular speech, jazz vocabulary, black idiom and a masterful use of Chicano Caló. The creative manipulation of jazz and other musical idioms as a basis for the heavily syncopated rhythms in many of the cantos, chants, and poems provides a highly auditory experience. These are poems meant for oral recitation rather than for silent private reading. Another distinctive element is the developed visual imagery in the narrative sequences of many of the poems. Both the auditory and visual components serve to concretize the experiences which form the matrix of Salinas's poetic material.

Ancillary to the dominant themes are those of identity, freedom, exile, and love. Wishing to reach his audience on both aesthetic and ideological levels, Raúl Salinas has consciously chosen to write partisan political poetry even as he explores the imaginative possibilities of his craft. As an artist he has taken sides and aligned himself with various social struggles of his time. It is this commitment rather than aesthetic consciousness that defines him as an important political poet. His attitude and struggles to gear his life towards the creation of a free and humane society are as valuable a contribution to contemporary Chicano literature as his luminous poetry.

Tomás Ybarra-Frausto

Dedicatoria

PA'
mi jefita
FRANCISCA
for
the turn-on.

Amá, whether you read
this or not;
Here's hoping
it makes up
for
the graduation picture
(cap/gown & diploma)
that never graced
your class-confusing
cuarto de sala.
Also, for the
lack of first-after-
basic training
photos proving
involvement in
immoral wars.
and for the
boxing trophies
i won/
lost at the pawnshop
to cure incessant
(almost incurable)
illness, may this
book gather dust
on your shelf.

SIEMPRE

to the convicted Sister/Brotherhood
y los pueblos del mundo
que luchan por ser libres.

"Tapón" y "Búfalo," Austin, Tejas, early '50s.
Foto: a street photographer.

Part 1

The Captive Years, 1957-1972

Raúl Salinas (left) with unidentified fellow prisoners in Leavenworth federal penitentiary, circa 1971.

Hey! World!!!*
. . . by way of self/me presento . . .

"hoping not to conjure up visions of ogres & monsters in your mind, i'm a 37 yr. old, 3rice-convicted, narcotics (offended!) offender. Sounds like some kind of nasty, no? i'm also a human being. What little i know was acquired through self-study. Therefore, not too swift, really. All my confined days/months/years, spent going to school. Which isn't saying too much for this country, its educational system and penitentiaries; or any combination of the three. However, in the solace of my cell i have held discourse with some of the tougher scribes, bards, free-thinkers, maddening spirits and revolutionary minds. It hasn't been an easy task, and surely don't know what they're ALL about, but it has kept the boogey-man away."

"That you enjoyed the poem, pleases me muchly, because it is your poem . . . belongs to everyone who can relate to/identify with/ see themselves in it. Such was the intended goal. i think! To present una experiencia personal which the reader could in turn transform (y vice versa) into a life's experience, the Chicano experience. Nay! The Universal experience! . . ."

"tus palabras llegan/ hacia mí/ como agua fresca/ olor a tierra/ en cántaros de barro/ como astros brillantes que iluminan/ la obscuridad de esta inmensa pajarera/ derritiendo en instantes numerosos/ las rejas de/ amargura y soledad/ . . ."

". . . as for my writings / solo son clamores que brotan / del fondo de la experiencia/ como azucenas casi-sofocadas/ por hierbas malas/ . . ."

". . . 3/3/'72—¡Pinches Putos! Me negaron publicar un article sobre 'censorship in prison.' ¡Ya me traen! Daily harassment. Primero el corte de greña, then the confiscation of the revista with the article on

---

*Excerpts from "Correspondencias de un reo," unpublished prison letters.

Genaro Vásquez' death . . ."

". . . pardon my delay in not writing any sooner, but the abrupt transition was Mind-Boggling! Punitive Transfer is the term used by our keepers. We refer to it as 'estirando cadena' (pulling chain) or 'shipping out.' Just a matter of semantics, i guess. Pero, anyway, aquí estamos . . ."

"It was quite an accident that we read about the GO-DOWN at Leavenworth, in the K.C. Star. Is there any move by CORA members to respond, giving an INTERNAL perspective? Can you get us equal space to give a more accurate account? That was a very cheap way of deceiving the public as to who the real villains were in that little HUMAN drama / tragedy. We feel that we can objectively focus on some issues, that unfortunately were not covered by that story . . ."

"Now, more about where we're at, what's (not) happenin' & what we're into. Geographically, i'm more lost now than i've been in the past 5 calendars. We are conveniently hidden away in the midst of a wild game reserve, somewhere in the boonies of So. Illinois. It's an antiseptically clean; architecturally innocent; physically oppressing joint! On the surface, this most maximum secure Alcatraz of the '60s & '70s appears loose and relaxed. But beneath its fake facade there is all manner of electronic surveillance equipment, modern chemo/psycho-therapy experimentation, and a variety of ridiculously sickening pacification programs . . ."

". . . big boost in moral knowing that most of the CORA members at Leavenworth have returned to 'normal' status. Can we expect an issue of AZTLAN, by the Frente Segundo, soon? THEY finally realized we were being effective. ¿Qué no? We agree, the paper MUST remain alive. The brothers can keep it so . . ."

" . . . regarding the article to counter the prison's white-wash job of a couple of months past, we think it needs doing. If you have the STAR clipping, send xeroxed copy of same. The reporter's name was Harry something-or-other. What do you intend to do from out there . . .?"

" . . . if you get to thinkin' we're imposin' too much (which we are), my only excuse is that we are under total lockdown, subjected to periodic gassing and brutal attacks. No access to personal/legal materials, nothing at our disposal, but each other. You know why. Please remember us to the brothers in that dungeon's inner caves . . ."

"Wed. July 26, 1972, this is the 3rd day of round-the-clock raids, also the anniversary of the Moncada assault in Cuba. There are 78 men confined in H-Block and 72 of us here in I-Block, both isolation units. Still incommunicado, more brothers still coming in. Sack lunches make up our 3 squares, and there's no squares for those into nicotine. Through slits in the window we look out towards the main corridor and see the 'inmates' obediently & domestically content, going to work. Mass confusion. We found a cigar amid debris of personal belongings-gone-to-the-trash. Miranda, Beto, Mares & me light it, pass it from cell to cell, each taking a puff and letting out rebel yells in salute of the eventual triunfo en el Caribe . . ."

"Our feelings are mutual, regarding the Puerto Rican Nacionalistas in their struggle for liberation. We stand to express these sentiments as strongly as we do for our Chicano/Mejicano peoples of the Southwest & Mejico. We have many times felt that not enough priority has been given to your patriotas . . . we are prepared (given our close proximity & encaged situation) to render assistance on their behalf, when called upon to do so . . ."

"Concerning the situation here, I'll give you a general rundown, so as not to incur the wrath/ill-will of the mailroom mutilators, any more than I already do. This is the public info: as of 7/23/72, approx. 150 prisoners were placed in isolation following a work stoppage in protest of the senseless beating of a Chicano prisoner . . ."

" . . . 9/1/72—Beto was taken to the 'boxcars' this morning. 1 lieutenant and 3 flunkies came for him. First, they made him stick his hand though the food tray slot in the bars, then they proceeded to handcuff him, opened the door and took him away. Strong brother, incredible development, carries himself well. All was quiet after that. Only float-

23

ing rumors to haunt us. As brother George used to say: 'things just ain't right, tonight' . . ."

". . . ¡Bartolina! Since July 17, we've been hidden from the sun. También los demás en el otro cantón. A según mis calculations, hoy es Sept. 11, 1972 . . ."

". . . as for the intended presentación of my poet-protégé, we must take a raincheck, no time for poetics, he's the one got bopped on the noggin. We've been here 8 weeks, so it's hard to predict anything. We go to court on our lawsuit against the prison, next week, too. Something's gotta give. Hope it ain't us! Ha-ha! . . ."

"Confined in isolation, a distortion of the senses begins to take place. One's equilibrium goes all out of kilter, after awhile. A veces me levanto del bonque y me mareo. Or like, i may catch a dark spot on the floor with the corner of my eye, as i write, and it'll seem to move. No creas que se me están volando. To write, i lay a blanket on the floor, availing myself of the light coming in through the bars of my cell, from the catwalk. When i start getting restless, i walk the length of my cell from front to back, over and over again. Ahora comprendo porque los animales de la selva hacen pace back and forth in their cages en el zoo . . ."

"Sabías que Mando me había offered assistance in 'raising' from my unexpired bit down yonder, no? . . . kited me a couple days ago. Piensa puede conseguir mi libertad from the 'pinches-rinches'. !Quién sabe! Lo malo es que, si continúan arrinconándome mucho más estos perros, voy a explotar. At this stage de mi vida, i'm going to have some difficulty containing my rage. No sé if i can ever be too happy anymore, when & if, i do raise . . ."

"If forced to continue living like an animal, soon—very soon—i'll be reacting like one. The consequences may be fatal, but the debt has been PAID IN FULL! There's no more to collect . . . they took 5 yrs of my life down there for $5 worth of smoke. 15 yrs is PREposterous!!! i'll fight it at all levels, i ain't going . . ."

"The long-drawn-out, no nothing scribblings of the 8th were the result of an extremely frustrated state of mind. You shouldn't be subjected to such insane outbursts; but, who else? If nothing more, it provided you a peep into another facet of my erratic personality. A glimpse of a man in his weak moments. Essential moments, if one is to remain undaunted in the face of adversity. i find the need to utilize these escape valves in my refusal to be broken by the enemy./ The spirit of Bro. George Jackson seems always close by/ . . ."

". . . yeah, the trial date coincided with the Tlatelolco Massacre's aniversario. That's all we rapped about with our non-latino comrades, in the chain bus, on our trip to town . . ."

"De eso se trata hoy en día, todos estudiando, concentrando en librar (como sea y como venga) a los presos/reclusos de aquí y del mundo entero . . ."

". . . un proceso de transformación mental; see it occurring, feel it surging within, it's at once amazing, extremely difficult to grasp, painful, and frightening!!!"

"Esto, junto con el caso ATTICA, y la muerte del compañero/maestro Jackson allá en QUILMAS, me agrava la mente. Me canso tanto a veces. Todo parece ser tan inútil. It's so frustrating, that in more desperate moments, nothing seems relevant, short of an all out confrontation, which would only prolong the prison wars, and claim more lives . . . which we can't afford to lose. Organizing time . . ."

"Se habla de los campos de entrenamiento por los desiertos del Amman, Jordan y en las provincias de Corea al norte. Nos interesa la vía popular que ha escogido el pueblo chileno y los hechos de la Nueva Cuba. Sobre todo esto, sigue la batalla propia . . . la lucha interna . . ."

"The reason why most of this letter is in english is because Mr. Hart & Mr. Hendrickson have prohibited me from corresponding in Spanish . . ."

25

". . . P.S.—due to the strange, foreign language imposed within this cage, your (this) letter will be: censored in isolation (for subversive code messages) sent to the mailroom censor (for possible sniffing) before going to my weeks-old caseworker, who is atrociously limited in any language, who will turn it over to a spanish-speaking guard (for final rubber-stamping) before (if ever) it reaches you. This information is legitimate, it comes from my caseworker. Our lawyer knows this is being sent. Let me know as soon as you receive it, if you do. P.S. No. 2—It's not our fault some folks ain't smart enough to know 2 & 3 languages, huh? . . ."

"Do keep in touch, you are the only outlets for expression & some of the few breezes of liberation that reach my asphyxiating cave. Until we exchange words again, yours in struggle . . ."

raúlpoeta

Poema Pa' Mi Cell-Partner

En aquel abismo
tan profundo y negro,
donde han caído nuestras almas;
siempre entra un rayo de luz.

Allí donde la humanidad sana nos tiene,
como enfermos contagiosos,
en vez de aceptar la realidad.
¿O somos nosotros, los que no queremos aceptar?

El tratar de derrotar
esta inmensa pajarera ('que contiene aves de distintas
    variedades')
con pura fuerza física, es (ahorita) un poco imposible.
Sólo queda una esperanza.

Una tarde de invierno
los vine a conocer,
por sus escrituras
hoy me doy a saber.

El águila que nos tiene
                  así . . . aquí,
como pollos mecanizados
llenos de dolor;
no tiene el poder
verdadero de arrestar
la mente superior.

Un día las alas le cortaron
a un pobre pavo real
en su corazón había tristeza
por no poder volar.

Pero el día glorioso se acerca
en qu'el pavo (otra vez) irá a volar,
espero qu'esta ave si escoja
el mejor camino para navegar.

Se acabó ya la miseria,
¡Órale pavo, a preparar!
y pensar en los amores
con que vas a disfrutar.

Quizás haiga una llama opaca
en el corazón de aquella mujer
Quien te ofreció jardín de flores
con su amor de anteayer.

Al ascender el cielo azul
(lejos de este lugar)
sábelo que has cumplido una misión
en haber dejado mentes
llenas de inspiración.

Con ésta ya me despido
nomás como queriendo decir
que también pajarillos presos
tienen el derecho de vivir.

11:15:'58
E-Wing – SOLEDAD

My first poem

Lamento*

to the memory of Charles "Bird" Parker
8/29/20-3/23/55
(musical genius & soother of early societal wounds)

"Blackbird scudding
under the rainy sky,
how wet your wings must be!
and your small head how sleek and cold with water."
                    —Edna St. Vincent Millay

NIGHT AND DAY
    " . . . *you are the one*,"

ON AN ENDLESS FLIGHT
    FROM A MUSICAL JOURNEY INTO PERFECTION

"*only you beneath the moon*
    and under the sun . . ."

A WEARY BIRD, TORMENTED

                    FROM WITHIN

SOUGHT REFUGE IN AN ALIEN WORLD.

No human ear was there to heed
    his sad/plaintive/WAIL . . .
        a
                Golden
                Voice
                    was
                        laid
                            to rest.
                    SOLEDAD / 2/17/59

---

*An experiment in sound, to be read contrapuntally with lyrics of Cole Porter's "Night and Day" interwoven.

Declaration of a Free Soul
(después de un shakedown)

A living nothing
   in this world of stone
teeming with loathesome
   Guardians of the State.
i'd best prefer upon my back
   the stinging lashes
of the dreaded cat-o-nine
   than to have these lowly curs
which i abhor
   constantly gnawing at my tortured mind.
O' Heinous Gods
   who stand for LAW!
to you i shall not bow.
   i once knelt to my mother's God,
but NEVER, to the Likes of YOU!

SOLEDAD / 2/27/59

Child-Vision by the Colorado River

Once I was young,
yesterday, perhaps,

and walked the
riverbanks alone.

Coming upon
an old fisherman,

teaching his young son
the art
    of
baiting a hook;

i was overcome
    with
        Envy.

SOLEDAD
4/26/59

31

Emergence of a Poet
(self-realization)

*

Tee-Hee
look at me
i
c
a
n
pee
from
up
a
tree . . . !

SOLEDAD 6/19/59

Gloriana

Giver of life;
though she never did—
for in her white-flowered world
enveiled in silv'ry silks,
all time was lost,
and so was life—
at least for one.

Nevertheless, she faced her world
all dress'd in black, each night.
and when the dawn had laid
its blanket of mist upon the ground,
i saw her still;
wide-eyed and unabashed.
While about her,
               Flutes
                       Screamed
                           in
                               the
                                   Air!!!

SOLEDAD 7/9/59

33

To My Woman

Tonight:
i know you are lonely,
though you're not within my view;
for loneliness is that suffering
which you've been subjected to.

Lonely nights of burning thirst
your ravaged soul must bear,
and its sole consolation
will come from one lone tear.

But do not weep, O' lonely woman,
for surely you have known
that in my darkest hour,
i too, am alone.

SOLEDAD 7/13/59

A Glimpse of Lore (ca)

Upon gazing at these plastered walls
they do not seem white-washed to me.
Instead,
they are yellow and dirty
crumbling with Time.

Silently i listen to the winds.

Sounds of Gypsy Guitars
possessed by the clouds overhead
convey in the form of sunbeams
natural folk-songs to cling to my ears.

Yes, Federico;
your presence is near me this day.
So near that i can see
your glowing eyes and radiant face;
unlike that puzzled youth of old,
who endlessly wandered 'til he got lost
in a sickening jungle of concrete and steel.

It is no different today, my friend.
The scenes are the same as you felt them.
Nothing has changed, García Lorca. Oh, yes!
        they are more revolting.
The skins of the tigress now come in two shades:
        purple and green
with contrasting stripes of blue and brown.
i vomit at the sight of the tigers in pink.

The rivers are told when to flow
the blue skies have now turned grey . . .
they burn the eyes.
You are better off dead.
Flash!
pistol shots ring in the humid & still afternoon,
dying Lorca
the jungle once before us floods in pools of blood,
jackal jackboots crush
          tender poetic countenance
Federico García Lorca;
and it is late in my afternoon.

                              SOLEDAD 7-(18-19)-59

Quise (Casi-Soñar) Soneto

pa' mi jefe
(whom i hardly know)

Quizás, some day when you are dead and gone
recordaré nights roaming empty streets, alone;
buscándote por los numerous bars
discovering years later i was just chasing stars.

Al encontrarnos in that distant land
quisistes embrace me, i offered my hand.
Bien me recuerdo that night when we met,
eres un perfect stranger i'll never forget.

We were perplexed by that tragic affair
as we sought to renew that which never was there.

SOLEDAD
8-(14/15)-59

37

(IN OTHER WORDS, i'd just as soon . . .)

for a prison guard
hated by everyone who knew him

O' Ruthless Rodent, please tell me,
why do you hate Humanity?
i pity you in your bitterness,
for you know not the ESSENCE of happiness.
Even i laugh now and then,
but then again, mice are mice where Men are MEN.
When you seek for "cheese" within my cell
and you find nothing, i can tell;
i just look at your face and if it looks bad,
i laugh to myself 'cause i know you are mad.

If i had a mousetrap as big as a house,
i'd relieve you of your misery:
        miserable
        MICKEY MOUSE.

                    SOLEDAD 1959
                    (in some kind of hurry)

Justification: A Discourse with Myself
(después de otro shakedown)

Remember how you cried
    when your castles in the sand
came tumbling down?

Unkindly,
    i snickered, and thought it cute
to hurt you.

Years later, i also feel like crying/
    cannot cry!
(even this, i'm not allowed to do.)

Had i only known
    the torment/discontent
that shattered
    house/castles/cells
can bring,
    i would've never, ever tried
to crumble/stumble on
    creative torres,
pretty minarets, laboriously built.

Today my "castle" is also being razed
    by merciless battering ram.
Down goes the palace, harem & King;
    Gone is the Princess . . . .

    Gone Everything!

The Walls / Huntsville
6-63

39

The Pisser
(solitary confinement)

Reeking antiseptic smells arise
    that nostrils cannot stand,
a changing of the Guard.
The clangour of steel-plated doors,
    and others yet to come . . . with bars . . . they say.
A Dixie cup (for what?) a piece of tissue 4x4 (enough?)
A musty, mildewed blanket on the floor.
    In the left-hand corner of
    this cruddy catacomb . . . a pit!
An excavation that disposes excremental waste.
    "Hey! Yew awright in there, boy?"
Like bats accustomed to the night
    the eyes begin to grope
for darkened shadows on clammy, concrete walls.
Instead, erotic fantasies cavort within my mind,
    competing with the silence that prevails
throughout the grotesque vacuum of this grotto.
After constant usage of the Hole,
    the lifeless blanket floats . . .
much in the manner of those dead souls
    littered upon the waters of
        Cocytus
            in Hades long ago.
"Git up, here's yore bread 'n' water!"
Cries of succor make flesh quiver up in spasms,
    as gods of sorts are agonizingly invoked
        (Aztec ones, in this case),
but straining, screaming voices
    have no sound
        and thus
            are never heard.

Las Paredes / Huntsville, 1964

40

DOS por UNO

(1)

They're gone, the routed avenues of all escape
Eventually, the soul must Seek to Hide,
Curtailing further intravenous rape;
And within Reality (that monster!) to collide.
The feast of Morpheus, once before:
Arteries that are fed no more.

(2)

Contemplation breeds.
Seeds are implanted.
Granted!

Nurtured thoughts are born.
Torn!
From their cranial womb.

6/4/64
Las Paredes
en
La Tejana
Huntsville, Tejas

Topic of Capricious/ Cantankerous Thought

for Henry Miller

"they" say you are a lecherous old man
i do not believe "them"
           my ears are accustomed to their lies
Boston Blue-Blood Bitches fear, dear sir,
           you might seduce their daughters
depriving them of (desiring) your
           verbal-vested phallus
Get down,
you swingin' satyr
           devour them all
. . . the hypocritical harlots . . .
and scratch their bony buttocks
           with
                     your
golden hooves!

The Walls / Huntsville
1964

Jazz: A Nascence

(Part I)

Spawn of coital bed
enjoyed by slave-ships & the sea,
   weaned in scarlet-red bordellos
suckling milk from Lulu White.

A raggi-tag-a-longin' kid
   behind So'thern funeral caravans;
stowaway up river
   with Satchel-Mouth & Joe the King.

Smothered with caresses
in crazy Town of Winds;
   reward for shyness lost:
Big Apple . . . Pie for Youuuuuu!!!

(Chorus I)

(solo)

   Late night SHRIEKING Sounds!
     commence
sweeping out the mental cobwebs
awakening brains from their torpor
tonal (poem) cascades
     Gently
washaway
musty/ dust settled within
thin lines of genius/ madness.

O' JazzBird fluttering in the darkened sky,
the willows have shed their tears too long
does no one hear their mournful cry?

(out)

La Tejana / Huntsville 1964

43

(. . . on reading of J. Frank Dobie's blasting the Texas Institute of Arts & Letters on behalf of John Rechy and his novel CITY OF NIGHT . . .)

Lightning Steed Immaculate:

the color of fresh-fallen snows
upon the range;

my glimpse of you was from a distance far,
yet you stood out,
controlling your terrain.

When sunlight first bestowed
its dawning kiss
on bleached caliche rocks,
those sacred plains
    of would-be captors
were left with etchings of your hoofs,
    Wild Stallion to the core.

Racing beyond the steep montañas, to the sun,
a gallant figure slowly dims & fades away,
but for a tiny speck on the horizon;
    Proud Mustang, you are Free.

                              Las Paredes de
                              La Tejana en
                              Huntsville
                              11/2/64

44

Epiphany

(a reading by UMKC poets)

i heard some black cats blow today
    who spoke of pigs, of being free, of many things.
No Shakespeare/Keats/ or Shelley, they;
    no bullshit sonnets of nobility & kings.

Oh, No!
Theirs was street poetry/turn on poesy
    of the wake-up kind;
with snap-to-it rhythm
    the type that blows your mind.

"Tighten up your game"/ "Get your head together"
    they said to me.
"NOW IS THE TIME for all oppressed humans to be set
                        free."

Eric Dolphy knew
    & Malcolm too;
O' yass, they did!
    while cowardly/some crawled in holes
and HID.

And so with clenched-fist i salute them:
Boss Bitchin' Black Bards!
Spread out the deck and deal 'em,
it's time to play some cards.

(afterthought)

the MAN'S stepped on our toes his final hour
from now on he should get
steady bombardment of our
People's Power.

                U.S. Penitentiary / Leavenworth / 1968

Tragedy

Lights out . . .
      Silence reigns for infinite seconds.
A smokers' chorus strikes the note,
      Hacking coughs in phlegmatic unison.
The sacred hour is upon us.

THE MASTURBATORS COME TO LIFE!!!

"Say, man! Keep those sheets from rustling
      i can't concentrate with all that noise!"

      Creaky springs, heavy sighs;
      ONAN swings & DUJI dies!
      Exploding peonies for no queen,
      wasted seed, that will not poets be.

Comes morning
      and starched socks
            (all peter'd out)
                  adorn the cell bars . . .

Frozen icicles for the orderly.

                            Leavenworth/1968

Meth-odically Speaking

(after 9-day bout with "Chicken Powder")

crawling out
        of concrete cubicles
sputum hanging
        bat-like
in cavernous throats.

Mouth-wracked
        (wreaked)
& dreary (bleary), heavy-eyed
        re-Born
one mo' time,
        in the first hours
of
    DAWNDAY.

SPEEEEEEEEEDDDDDDD!!!

coursing up/down veins
        abused
and long-collapsed;
buzzzzing & churnnnning & whirrrrrrling
        FLASHES
of
    ve-
        lo-
            ci-
                ty!!!

Come
      down
decrescendo
      organ-ic shrivels
bone marrow sucked
      out
of tune
SOON IT WILL BE OVER WITH.

           Cell 505   B-Wing
           Leavenworth/69

In Memoriam: Riche

And he died . . .
        2 years later—
in the putrefying bowels
        of a dismal prison—
death's impact
        SLAPS!
the face of consciousness
        and jars the torpid brain
AWAKE!

        Farewells were said
in other
        Caverns of Detention
when winds of Freedom
        carried him away;
nevermore to be seen.

        Until, that is,
time came to lay him down
        to rest
and shovel earth over his corpse.

        (THE DEATH-KNELL CAUSES FLESH
TO SHUDDER ONCE AGAIN)

Kayo, lying rigid in the streets
        which were his playground;
the rains found him
        and blessed
his lifeless bones.
        Inflated beyond limit,
tender veins became balloons
        that burst too soon,
his heart was stilled.

And so, dear friend & brother,
     The System
     (not God!)
          created you . . .
that system
     took
       you
         away.

8/69
U. S. Penitentiary
Leavenworth

El Tecato
(Side 2)

*pa' los chavalitos de
Elías (Alex) Perales: "El Perro,"
camarada asesinado por los
narcos en 1967.*

He turned the page of Life
    each day
in the hours of ham 'n' eggs;

Performing sacred rituals,
ministering to his body's needs.
    The Morning Fix!
(particular fuel for most particular machine.)

Then off to hustle up the milk & bread;
the fix that 7 children would require.
And when sandman's gifts were rubbed
from hungry progeny's eyes,
        that scourge . . . that social leper
beamed with pride
        because he knew he could
(in spite of sickness)
        well provide.

Narcotic officers didn't think so,
        nor do i feel they cared.
And so one night they stalked their prey:
        a sick, addicted father/brother/son,
who recognized his children's need
        for food and nourishment
while no one recognized his need
        for drugs or treatment.

So the predators gunned him down
in the manner of that social madness
that runs rampant across the land,
dressing itself in the finery & raiments of
JUSTIFIABLE HOMICIDE!!!

El Once / Leavenworth / 1969

A Trip through the Mind Jail

LA LOMA

Neighborhood of my youth
demolished, erased forever from
the universe.
You live on, captive, in the lonely
cellblocks of my mind.
Neighborhood of endless hills
muddied streets—all chuckhole lined—
that never drank of asphalt.
Kids barefoot/snotty-nosed
playing marbles/munching on bean tacos
(the kind you'll never find in a café)
2 peaceful generations removed from
their abuelos' revolution.

Neighborhood of dilapidated community hall
—Salón Cinco de Mayo—
yearly (May 5/Sept. 16) gathering
of the familias. Re-asserting pride
on those two significant days.
Speeches by the elders,
patriarchs with evidence of oppression
distinctly etched upon mestizo faces.
"Sons of Independence!"
Emphasis on allegiance to the tri-color
obscure names: JUAREZ & HIDALGO
their heroic deeds. Nostalgic tales of war
years under VILLA'S command. No one listened,
no one seemed to really care.
Afterwards, the dance. Modest Mexican
maidens dancing polkas together
across splintered wooden floor.
They never deigned to dance with boys!
The careful scrutiny by curbstone sex-perts

8 & 9 years old. "Minga's bow-legged,
so we know she's done it, huh?"

Neighborhood of Sunday night jamaicas
at Guadalupe Church.
Fiestas for any occasion
holidays holy days happy days
'round and 'round the promenade
eating snowcones—raspas—& tamales
the games—bingo cakewalk spin-the-wheel
making eyes at girls from cleaner neighborhoods
the unobtainables
who responded all giggles and excitement.

Neighborhood of forays down to Buena Vista—
Santa Rita Courts—Los Projects—friendly neighborhood
cops 'n' robbers on the rooftops, sneaking peeks
in people's private night-time bedrooms
bearing gifts of Juicy Fruit gum for
the Project girls/ chasing them in adolescent heat
causing skinned knees & being run off for the night
disenchanted walking home affections spurned
stopping stay-out-late chicks in search of
Modern Romance lovers, who always stood them up
unable to leave their world in the magazines' pages.
Angry fingers grabbing, squeezing, feeling,
french kisses imposed; close bodily contact, thigh &
belly rubbings under shadows of Cristo Rey Church.

Neighborhood that never saw a school-bus
the cross-town walks were much more fun
embarrassed when acquaintances or friends or relatives
were sent home excused from class
for having cooties in their hair!
Did only Mexicans have cooties in their hair?
¡Qué gacho!
Neighborhood of Zaragoza Park
where scary stories interspersed with
inherited superstitions were exchanged
waiting for midnight and the haunting
lament of La Llorona—the weeping lady
of our myths & folklore—who wept nightly
along the banks of Boggy Creek
for the children she'd lost or drowned
in some river (depending on the version).
i think i heard her once
and cried
out of sadness and fear
running all the way home nape hairs at attention
swallow a pinch of table salt and
make the sign of the cross
sure cure for frightened Mexican boys.

Neighborhood of Spanish Town Café
first grown-up (13) hangout
Andrés,
tolerant manager, proprietor, cook
victim of bungling baby burglars
your loss: Fritos 'n' Pepsi Colas—was our gain
you put up with us and still survived!
You, too, are granted immortality.

Neighborhood of groups and clusters
sniffing gas, drinking muscatel
solidarity cement hardening
the clan the family the neighborhood the gang
¡NOMÁS!
Restless innocents tattoo'd crosses on their hands
"just doing things different"
"From now on, all troublemaking mex kids will be
sent to Gatesville for 9 months."
Henry home from La Corre
khakis worn too low—below the waist
the stomps, the greña with duck-tail
—Pachuco Yo—

Neighborhood of could-be artists
who plied their talents on the pool's
bath-house walls/intricately adorned
with esoteric symbols of their cult:

the art form of our slums
more meaningful & significant
than Egypt's finest hieroglyphics.

Neighborhood where purple clouds of Yesca
smoke one day descended & embraced us all.
Skulls uncapped—Rhythm n' Blues
Chalie's 7th St. Club
loud funky music/ wine spodee-odees/ barbecue & grass
our very own connection man: big black Johnny B—
Neighborhood of Reyes' Bar
where Lalo shotgunned
Pete Evans to death because of
an unintentional stare

and because he was escuadra,
only to end his life neatly sliced
by prison barber's razor.
Durán's grocery & gas station
Güero drunkenly stabbed Julio
arguing over who'd drive home
and got 55 years for his crime.
Ratón: 20 years for a matchbox of weed. Is that cold?
No lawyer no jury no trial i'm guilty
                    Aren't we all guilty?

Indian mothers, too, so unaware
of courtroom tragi-comedies
folded arms across their bosoms
saying, "Sea por Dios."

Neighborhood of my childhood
neighborhood that no longer exists
some died young—fortunate—some rot in prisons
the rest drifted away to be conjured up
in minds of others like them.
For me: only the NOW of THIS journey is REAL!

Neighborhood of my adolescence
neighborhood that is no more
YOU ARE TORN PIECES OF MY FLESH!!!!
Therefore, you ARE.
    LA LOMA—AUSTIN—MI BARRIO—
                    i bear you no grudge
i needed you then . . . identity . . . a sense of belonging
i need you now.
so essential to adult days of imprisonment,
you keep me away from INSANITY'S hungry jaws;
                    Smiling/ Laughing/ Crying.

i respect you having been:
my Loma of Austin
my Rose Hill of Los Angeles
my West Side of San Anto
my Quinto of Houston
my Jackson of San Jo
my Segundo of El Paso
my Barelas of Alburque
my Westside of Denver
Flats, Los Marcos, Maravilla, Calle Guadalupe,
Magnolia, Buena Vista, Mateo, La Seis, Chiquis,
El Sur, and all Chicano neighborhoods that
now exist and once existed;
        somewhere . . . someone remembers . . .

                     14 Sept. '69
                     Leavenworth

José Montoya

Journey II
for my son Ricardo

They're tearing down the old school
    wherein i studied as a child
        Our Lady of Guadalupe . . .
Parochial prison/Internment camp for
    underprivileged Mexican kids,
        soon to be pummelled by
merciless wrecking ball.
    What do i remember best?
    What childhood mem'ries
cling stubbornly to the brain
    like bubble-gum under a table?

        Saturday afternoon Confession:
(it was no sweat giving up the li'l tadpole sins,
    spittin' out the big bullfrogs was the hassle.)
with only shadowy profile of Padre José,
    ever ready to impose heavy
        Our Father/Hail Mary sentence.
Catechism: Doctrina classes after school
    First Holy Communion Day!
        (i ingest
one of many Sacraments to come
    & speak to the galaxies)
    white suit/ padrino Chris/ a ride in
        Posey's pre-war '38 Buick
The twins: Boffo & me fantasize,
    grown up—slaying dragons—planting corn
        if they would marry us.
Climbing, zooming heavenward, up rickety
    stairs into chamber of horrors/haunted
        house of learning . . . viewed by un-
suspecting boyzngirlz as Transylvanian
    castle of doom.
        "No, Minga, those weren't black

ghosts flying around on lofty 5th floor
        balustrade, just Sisters' penguin-like
                habits; hanging out to dry."
The unforgettable recital: tribute to John Phillip
        Sousa, in abandoned subterranean lunchroom.
                All dress'd up like cadets. i played the
triangle. Big deal! the seamstress goofed on
        my uniform. Each time triangle went . . . ting!
                . . . oversized trousers slipped down
another inch. Trusty blue/gray lunchbox:
        opened many a coin-slot
                on schoolyard bullies' heads.
Singing "God Bless America": would you believe?
        Competing for the lead with my friend Fernando . . .
the one who, like Nash & cousin Albino, never
        returned that Saturday; from gathering palms
                for Palm Sunday . . . crushed beneath grinding
locomotive wheels.
        How unreal it all seems now.
                They MUST have gone to heaven;
how could any God deny them entrance?
        Such beautiful people . . . young plants
                who never lived to blossom.
With their deaths life lost all meaning.
        Fernando: my competitor in song—Albino: cohort
                in chasing girls—Nash: (good ol' thoughtful
                                        Nash)
never once forgot my birthday
        How unfair . . . unkindly
                they were stripped from my being.
"If only good people go to heaven when they die,
        i done blew my chance of ever seeing them again."

                Strutting birdbreast stuck way out, smoking
WINGS cigarettes. Great big eyes for Juanita what's-
        her-name. Treating demure Catholic young ladies
                to unpaid-for Kress's 5 & 10 birthstone rings

inducing them to smoke . . . too soon busted! Reprimanded.
     Forced to kneel prostrate before giant crucifix and
     Sister Hermaneda. Tender knuckles kissed by
wooden ruler. Sorry, wrong rhumba.
     Carlin's place: our crowd o' rowdies jitterbugging
         me watching.
"You got to ac-cen-tuate the positive, e-li-mi-nate the
     negative, don' mess with Mr. In-Between."
         Sounds: Mercer, Woody & The Duke
"Couldn't make it without you, don't get around
     much anymore."
     A thousand merry harlequins dance happily/
nostalgically inside my head.
     The families whose sons 'n' daughters
         became priests & nuns.
i wonder what percentage of us
     turned nomadic children
         of the streets?

     AGNES MARIE: because you were who you were,
         i'd name a daughter after you. i still possess the
            comic valentine you sent me. The one of a
gawky/gangly gal in bathing suit & water-wings, which
read: "Lissen punk, you be mine or i'm sunk!"
         So many times i've seen you, as i turned a corner
         crossed a street, in so many different cities. But—
         unlike Dante's Beatrice—the you i saw was never
            really you.
         The 1st hip priest encountered—Father
                   Busch—
Father Green was, also, pretty much aware;
         in that long ago, before the era of NOW clergy-
                   men:
         BRIGANTI & GOERTZ.
"Polished Pebbles": worn-out operetta
         year-in-year-out performance by seniors
     at uptight Knights of Columbus Hall.

To this day i've yet to know
who penned that lame libretto of corn!

The sandpile in back of Joseph's Garage
the little pasture at the French Legation;
first experiments with sex conducted there.
Josie luring us to Confederate Cemetery
for advanced
lessons. i chicken out and run. So, wherever
you may be, J., i apologize,
i just wasn't ready.
Sister Armela:
i've got news for you;
Ivory Soap Don't Taste Worth A Damn!
And all i ever said was DAMN!!!
The busted water fountain which i didn't bust.
Ask God, He'll tell you i didn't do it.
Snitchin' Teresa said i did.
E-X-P-U-L-S-I-O-N!
Retaliation/Paintbrush in hand/no longer
dull abandoned lunchroom. Red paint on sickly-green walls.
Me an' my rappie—Joe Giddy—decorate the
dingy
cellar and defy the Gods.
"CATCH ME IF YOU CAN, YOU'LL NEVER TAKE ME
ALIVE,"—signed MR. X . . . "GOD IS DEAD AND BURIED
IN THIS DINER THAT NEVER FED ANYONE." "THE
EASTSIDE TERRORS STRIKE AGAIN."
Yeah, i did it,
you shoulda' never kicked me out, father.
i loved the school in my own way.
Even if it was mostly prayers, i still learned something.
There's still a couple of guys
i'm pretty tight with/ communicate with:
like
Ol' St. Jude Thaddeus, who's had Miz' Hill
on her knees these 36 years;

                    & St. Dismas, he's one of the fellows.
He KNEW what was happening!
There's more . . . much more . . . an infinite voyage
              on a route paved with invaluable gems
                  to treasure forever.
When i was out last time, i visited the old school
              once again. It had changed some. A section of
                  the old spook house facade was gone, a
                          modern
cracker-box was in its place. i would have lingered
            to catch a few vibrations of that other world,
                      but
            i was a sick poet that day. My only concern
was the 4 caps of medicine someone had left under
        a rock for me. i thought of going back the next
                      day.
        A prior commitment with the courts of law
made this impossible.
     i won't be there for the razing,
        but i'll return when i'm an aged, wizened
                man.
When freedom doves are on the wing again,
        i must go back and savor long the taste
           of spirits from another era (long before
the fall of innocence), upon my famished heart.

        And if there is a parking lot
          erected on that sacred spot

i'll blow it up with dynamite

        and think of everything
          it meant to me.

        Leavenworth / 70

Pregúntome

where does it all lead to?
i mean, like where are we going?
and where did we come from?
where did it all begin?
and who started it?

is the problem social/
            cultural/
                    political/
                            economical?

is revolution a sole solution?
or what?

whom do we attack, and must we?
are the panthers at fault/
      the weather underground/
            los indios/
                    or the mexican people?
when does a rainbow coalition take place,
      and where?
does aztlán mean utopia?
do we sacrifice our leaders?
do we burn high priest at the stake,
and light the pyre with soul on ice?
but that's a black/white problem.
i shouldn't be concerned
but i am.

just like i'm concerned about bernadine & angela
    and carlos montez & gío
like the bombings concern me.
    and the highjackings
y la marcha de la reconquista
    and mayday concern me.
so much to learn . . . so much to do.
    the man's got an easy job
no wonder he finds such willing recruits,
    Always!

USP—Leavenworth / 1970

Ciego/Sordo/Mudo

pa' un coco

Simón, man;
awakening from a
deep & non-euphoric dream
nausea overcame me.

    A tacotío (that grano asquerzo
    which affects our piel de bronce)
    tells me i've been dreaming
    the American Dream . . .

        No way, compa, this
        was a righteous nightmare!
        Besides, ESTÁS MÁS LUCAS
        TÚ QUE LA CHINGADA!

In that nightmare/dream sequence
i delight in being patriotic/chauvinistic/
middleclassamerican. LOOK MA,
I'M A JONES BOY DRIVIN'
A 69 CHEEVIE.

    i don't wanna be a meskin all my life—
    "There's equal opportunities for all,
    my son, just go out and
        LOOK."

O' the landlord
               he is pounding
& my creditors are
               hounding
soon uptightness
               starts resounding
FOUND: an opportunity to go out
               boosting
               dealing dope
               & robbing banks.

"Yeah, one good score and
i'll move away from this
stinkin' barrio into the suburbs."

I Sentence You To The Federal Penitentiary . . .

Hay! Amigo, Como Se Llamas—Soy Purro
                       Misicano,
Tacolos, enchiluders, equal rights & all that
sorta' jazz.   Later for you, Chump!
YOU ARE ALREADY DEAD AND BURIED,
WITH NO ONE TO MOURN YOU!!!

U. S. Penitentiary—Leavenworth
1970

Los Caudillos

Stifling
> Crystal City
>> heat

rouses Texas sleepers
> the long siesta finally over

at last, at long, long last
> politics wrested from

tyrannical usurpers' clutches
> fires are stoked

flames are fanned . . .

> conflagrating flames

of socio-political awareness.

> In rich Delano vineyards
>> Chávez does his pacifist thing

> "lift that crate
>> & pick them grapes"

> stoop labor's awright—with God on your side.

Small wonder David Sánchez
> impatient & enraged in East L.A.

dons a beret, its color symbolizing
> Urgent Brown.

> Voices raised in unison
>> in Northern New Mexico hills

> "¡esta tierra es nuestra!"
>> cached clutter: invalid grants/unrecognized treaties

> their tongues are forked,
>> Tijerina;

Indo-Hispano
> you're our man.

Denver's Corky boxing lackeys' ears back
        let them live in the bottoms for awhile
see how they like a garbage dump
        for a next door neighbor.

José Ángel Gutiérrez: MAYO's fiery vocal cat
        the world does not like energetic noisemakers
or so says papa henry b. (the saviour of San Anto)
        who only saved himself.

In Eastern Spanish Ghettos
        Portorro street gangs do
Humanity.

                Young Lords: (Cha-Cha, Fí & Yoruba)
                        burglarize rich folks' antibiotics
                rip off x-ray units/hospital
                        —become medics of the poor—
                ghetto children must not die
                        of lead poisoning & T.B.

Latin Kings: (Watusi Valez & the rest)
        if you're doing social service
how can you be on
        terrorizing sprees (with priest accompanist)
in near Northside Chicago?

        Ubiquitous? We're everywhere!

Arise! Bronze People,
        the wagon-wheels gather momentum.

Leavenworth
Oct. /'70

No Tears for Pearl

Desolate Pearl
   adrift on bigoted Gulf
Coast sands
   tainted
   marijuana
flower hung upon
the wall.
From nether regions
—out of desperation—
comes an unrestricted
       SOUND!
The strain
   was pain
too powerful for acned,
ugly-beautiful, tormented
SOUL.
It hurts an artist to
       destroy her/him self.
The strain
   was pain
an aura of drama
       ability to entertain.
Fair-skinned
       BESSIE
          reincarnate
veneration at the grave.
More! More! More!
       Frantic fans in frenzy
ask for guts to spill
       upon the stage.
who cares if you're lonely,
       the crowds want music . . .
they want your LIFE.

Let's do the Full-Tilt Boogie, gal!
Port Arthur's puritans embarrassed
   by the rhythm of the
      Siren's Song.
No more . . . gone Janis . . . raunchy you.
"Turtle Blues" remains tattooed
      forever on my eardrums.
Frizzled hair & boa caught/entangled
   on fast unwinding tape
choking / stifling / silencing
the whiskeyguzzling / hedonistic / superrockstar/
      HUMAN BEING.
too harrowing the Hungry Horse.

Leavenworth / 1971

Sinfonía Serrana

how can
i
sing you
songs of love

when all
i ever learned were
Howls of Hate

i
cannot gift you
with
bouquets of joy

my
garden only yields
wild
Weeds of Sorrow

you
asked for the sun
i
could not provide

the
blame is not yours
i
wanted the moon
i
cried for the moon

when the
wrappings came off
i found
plastic and sham

so
to nurse both
our wounds from the
thorns of deceit

we
will sign our
last love-pact
in blood

with
the scalpel of loneliness
i'll carve you a sliver
of my soul

to
paste up in
the scrapbook
of your heart

even
tho
i
know

poems
don't bring in
much money
these days.

Leavenworth / 1971

Overcoming a Childhood Trauma

for a couple of teachers
along life's way

I must not speak Spanish
in the classroom.

I must not speak Spanish on
the schoolgrounds.

I must not speak Spanish.

I must not speak.

I must not

O' yesss i willllll,

CHINGUEN A TODA SU MADRE!!!

Love,
Roy

Leavenworth / 71

First Visit to the Font

Ensconced
        for days and nights
in $3.00 motel room
        begetting love?
a pencil-tongue
        writes poetry
across crude caesarean scars
        of such sweet body's slate.
Eraser-like
        a mouth rubs out
stretch-marks, left on bulging breasts
        from many sucklings.

i eat
        you eat
                me/we
float on passion's seas
        drift off in slumber sounds
of Gloria Lynne & Bossa Nova.
        Awakened, 'Trane declares
                for US
A Love Supreme . . . A Love Supreme . . . A Love
                                        Supreme . . .

Months later, finding myself
        obsessed with you
(a worse habit to kick than heroin)
        i baptize you:

                    "DUJI"

                            Leavenworth / 1971

Nutmeg Nuances

We were (almost) children
        yesterday
we chose (do you s'pose?)
        our own insanity
refusing/ rejecting
        forms
forced & prescribed.

We chased fleecy lambs
        through
meadows 'n' pastures
        in the clouds.

We laughed
        an unrestricted
                (with no shackles!)
LAUGH!
at funny-people movies
human tragicomedies.

We rapped to
        SunFlower
who dared peek
        over prison walls
to welcome the SUN.

Later we learned
she was sentenced
by sadistic tower guard
(for consorting/ conversing
        with two humanoids:
                one black/
                        one brown
                                or red?)
to be chopped down at sunset
aren't they weird?

We communed with nature
        yesterday
so we know THAT'S wrong,
        (the part about the guard, i mean.)
yesterday
we were being children
        (the warden forbid!)
we were for-reals.

USP—Leavenworth
1971

News from San Quentin
(August 21, 1971)

A Tender Warrior
       fell today
victim
       of the JAIL MACHINE!!
And in Leavenworth Prison
       rank right-on-ers
of the chilly clenched fist set
       (complete with afro-do)
dig soul music, man . . . Soul Music!
       & dream of
              one
                    more
                          Kadillac!
Those few
       who have been touched
              by
              MADNESS
in silent darkness pray
       to the spirit of Ho Chi Minh
and grow impatient/ intolerant
       of the oppressed . . .
those who wish to stay that way.
       There's no turning back for us.

A Tender Warrior
       fell today
a flame that burned for
       revolutionary eons

was doused/
      slowly ebbed its glow.
We all grew a bit today,

      brother george.

Our struggle became more intense!

      Leavenworth / 71 / (strange things beginning to O-cur!)

Sojourn Down the Styx
(a glimpse of Hell)

Part III

The charnel-house awakens.
        toilets flush
and pent-up fears/ frustrations/
        poison & desires,
float out: Missouri River-bound.
        Soul Music!
piped-in nirvana
        for pre-conditioned pawns.
i wake to coffin
        made of
bars & locks & wire & walls & GUNS;
        while every pore and fiber
in my still mobile cadaver
        screams out
        for
        Liberation!

And my children?
        Esos niños:
        Ricardo, Eleanor y Lorenzo.
Yes,
they joyfully romp
        through the timeless
        corridors of my tormented mind
(when i allow myself the pain).
Those seedlings sowed
        somewhat carelessly
        (with love):
now tended (dotingly)
        by one-half
the initial harvesting crew.
        Unfortunately

clocks don't run backwards
                    nor does youth
raise from its prison death
                    to mock grey hairs
nor mourn society's accusations
                        of unfatherliness.
(Dolores Ibarruri, i remember your sacrifice.)
We reach out
& teach.
Out of the depths of degradation & despair
out of experiences forged in terror and in fear,
we hope for better sons & daughters,
to grow stronger than iron bars and walls of stone.
As strong as spears & lances & machetes;
                as strong and deadly
                    as the assault rifle
                      of
                FREEDOM.

                        Leavenworth
                        Late '71

Enorme Transformación . . .

hoy me traes enloquecido
rugiendo como un león
en jaulas de odio y soledad.

Enorme Transformación
que de un nopal
ya casi-moribundo
has dado fruto
a tan ardiente árbol
sin cesar.

Enorme Transformación
hoy me das a conocer
que no tan sólo yo . . . soy el que sufro.
el compañero con su piel obs-
cura,
o aquel un poco mas pálido
que yo,
también él sufre
si es oprimido
bajo explotación.

Enorme Transformación
que me hace comprender
que el vietnamita es balaceado
el negro pisoteado
y el latino encarcelado.

Por eso en estos días
          empiezo a sentir
                    mi liberación
cual se me está concediendo
          sobre
                    esta
ENORME TRANSFORMACIÓN.

Leavenworth / Noviembre '71

Chan / Dan-Go

to my wigged-Out crony
from "Naptown"
Robert Chandler/ alto
saxophonist supreme

i heeaaard . . .
A
FREEDOM JAZZ DANCE!!!
            Do
                U
                    recalls
the false-
                ifying fakes
                    (shakes of the head received)
who'd bring ol' Leaven' to a "screeching halt"?
U scairt them false prophets,
                Third,
Blk. RE/ evolutionary of jazz;
                armed with the AXE of truth.

No Bet!
    The Blooz is:
Sequestered Saxophones bespeaking TRUTH
                & gassed-out guitars committing suicide.

Buddha & Trane saw it coming, and laid it; remember?
Feeling Pharaoh's KARMA through chanting Leon . . .
                /and Boone?

Soon, Chan-man, soon;
        to feel de mud
between de toes;
        Den goes . . .
& sing our songs
        of Liberation.

                                    marion prison
                                    may 2, 1972
                                    (amid rumblings of
                                      impending
                                          DOOO . . . M!!!!)

Part 2

Poems of (Partial) Freedom, 1972-1979

Comentario

Mi carnalito Raúl tiene fama entre la "sparse palomilla" aquí en el rincón del noroeste, por aparecer en cualquier lugar muy de repente. Hasta se le pusó "El Brown Leprechaun" por esa manía. Así es que nos topamos yo y este chavo, and because of it, neither one of us (and a LOT of people, either!) has been the same ever since.

Tapón popped into our midst while we were occupying El Centro in Winter of '72, helándonos las . . . and trying to keep warm with Mexican anti-freeze. Right away, it was a "truly love political," entre la gente y el poeta. Así como cada día seguimos recobrando lo nuestro, no hay duda pa' nosotros que sin el "Roy," no habríamos todavía recobrado la poesía como un arma importante que nuestra gente siempre ha usado en contra 'el enemigo.

Como arma, Salinas has honed his work both into a deadly instrument of capitalist indictment and an instrument of unity of all struggling people—but especially Indios y Raza. What distinguishes a mi hermano from many other poets is that he has been part of creating that struggle and not merely recording it. From the prison wars, studying with Puerto Rican nationalist prisoners, to riot squad confrontations facing Raza and Blacks in the streets and B. I. A. pigs on the river, the building of homes in Socialist Cuba and then . . . the painful and lonely job of creating it into art.

I am privileged to have been part of much which is contained in "Poems of (Partial) Freedom." I've SEEN that beautiful, creative process that draws on the deepest and best of our people. I have seen, heard, and felt "Taps" give it all back to them at occupations, demonstrations, arroyos & cañones, universities, peñas, pintas, daycare

91

centers, migrant slave camps, barrios, ghettos, Indian reservations y el río Nisqually.

Por eso, "Un Trip . . . y Otras Excursions" is long overdue, and would have been in print hace mucho, were it not for all the innumerable demandas made on him por el pueblo. These demands, he has willingly undertaken to meet—at the expense of multiple mountains of unpublished manuscripts. An additional contribution in El Centro's long and grueling history committed to building a more social and humane world community. Pués ya sabes, "Slim," nos rayamos when you "popped up" at the Centro . . . tu poesía dice lo demás.

Roberto Maestas
El Centro de la Raza
Seattle, Washington
March 29, 1977

Crash Landing

. . . by way of fragments, first impressions, momentary madness, waves
of warmth, lingering poisons, solid good-feeling flashes, and plain old
sofocadas . . .

And this is Seattle
 Where virgin snows
  provide the bed
where mountains & the clouds
 hold intercourse.
Prison-deadened senses
 (latent touch)
  respond
dancing & prancing
 merrily along
  to the tune of
(partial)
 FREEDOM.
Like myriad bits 'n' pieces
 splinters
  broken
crystal-clear cut glass,
 Image of HERE
  are
skittered-scattered
 throughout my total being.
  Like so many scrambled marbles?
And this is Seattle . . .
 Where lands end
 on Pacifica's Northwestern shores.
Where the palomía is sparse
 (although i dug some cotorriando)
Time out for "TIME OUT"
 1 bombed-out, zapped moment
  in limbo
held down by the pressing thumb

                    of the
                    UNKNOWN
Followed by flowing, fluid
        gentle reflections:
                poetic seagulls
                        soaring on the Sound.
And this is Seattle . . .
        Where good Brown-Cinnamon-
                Nutmeg-Canela smiles
comfort/nurse   wounds old & new
        inflicted by the savage beast.
Where
        Toña
                Sacred Secret Amulet
Charm of profuse
                Miracles & magic
                sleeps in mausoleums of lore
and understands (i hope!)
        my weird/warped concepts of love.
Where infant's laughter
        & caressing rains
                prove therapeutic balm.
The Toilet Snores
        while the captivating woman
                SisterLoverFriend
                        and i
Share (in each other's loneliness)
        one more HA-HA for the road.
                Still:
Mi alma yearns for Austin,
        my Cora burns for India
                therefore, my psyche
                        reads Aztlán.
And this is Seattle . . .
        where all the fantasías & dreams
                of Long-Ago
came tumbling/fumbling down

ECSTATIC ERO-WAVES.
Where the snows melted
        & anxious avalanche
                gave way
to the lost/lust jungle
                (of equatorial temperatures)
where mating was raw, pure, unleashed & good.
Then, congealed again
                (forever?)
                        within the icy mass/mess.
¡Pinche Vida!
        ¿Por qué me sigues dando tanto costalazo?
Still . . . i walk Seattle's streets
        while in the shooting gallery
                in my gourd
constant bombardment of Pintos
                (integral links on my shackles)
        profes (but no poets) . . . (until Flaco
                                showed in town)
                friends
                        companion colleagues
                                unlovers
                                LIFE.
Yea! The poet functions
                        for the 1st time
                        in the
                                WORLD!
And this is Seattle . . .
        Where Human-Ness
                (especially among
                        the young)
peeks through
                prevailing & pervading rains
                        of soaking loneliness
                                (no longer therapeutic).
Hash-Grass enshrouded atmosphere
        prevails/avails

in lonely, aged, mid-Victorian
                    hotel room
(mi celda solitaria)
                    while insects gambol
                    through poems long neglected.
    y lucha continúa
                    & i so incapacitated/crippled
porque me falta aquel . . . aquello
                    necesario pa' que vibre el corazón.
And this is Seattle . . .
                    of early Springtime
                    Sunday cruises
into peaceful Seward Park
                    of green paisajes
Where Berna (La Manita)
                    comforted our moans & groans
                    our lovesick blues
as we soothed the soreness
    (al estilo)
                    with vironga/grass & down-home
                    Sounds
                    of Little Joe.
Y la música de Sunny
                    (constant reminder)
" . . . los hombres no deben de llorar
                    pero te vengo llorando . . ."
strengthening (with mates thought lost)
                    a truly love political.
And this is Seattle . . .
                    where Northwest Piojos
                    (Social insects con raíces en Aztlán)
nip & bite at people's consciousness
                    with teatro de los camposbarrios
                    condición y situación
presenting to the gente
                    nuestra obvia realidad
& still had time to say:

¡Bienvenido cucaracho!
            take him in their fold.
And this is Seattle . . .
        where Beacon Hill
                (farol del pueblo)
keeps vigil
                over
sick, corrupt (and apathetic) civic cliques
        Y El Centro de la Raza
                becomes a REALITY.
Centro where tri-ethnic vibes
        permeate/create
                class-consciousness
                        among the poor.
Where lessons in LIFE
        are taught daily
                (by Revolutionary Sisters/
                        Dedicated Daughters)
on lawns untended
                due
to energies spent
        en el rescate & self determination
                of the oppressed.
Where 3rd World fuerzas
        se unen
                & deal with:
                        Nicaraguan disasters
                        Indian genocide (of modern-day
                                        massacres)
                        Plantation life of campesinos
                        Movimiento Estudiantil
                        Black Construction slaves
                        Presos Políticos (y sociales)
                        Y raza Raza RAZA
in unyielding solidarity.

And this is Seattle . . .

But somewhere beyond
            Majestic Mount Rainier
in dungeons built by evil men
        are brothers/sisters (prisoners)
            who are still not free
As i am still not free . . .
        though i walk Seattle's streets.

Seattle, Washington
Nov. 27, '72—May 3, '73

Tragedia

For years

    (imprisoned)
           i
      made love
        to
      paper-playmates.

Now

    (out in the world)
           i
      find the need
        to
      paste my woman
         on the wall
        before i ball

           HER
in
   the
     palm
        of
          my
            hand.

Seattle
January 1973

100

SOooooo-REeeeeeAaaaal Poem

Umbrellas
mournfully kissed
by sad-eyed tears of rain

Strut 'round the compound
wearing
tractor-tread brogans,
A la (diurnal somambulist) mode
ZOM——BEEZ!

¿y
yo?
Comsumiendo tomos y volúmenes académicos
vomitando, (all the while)
venenos de antiguas cárceles;
Haciendo cerebro voy:
Sobre cuál arma escoger
Contra esta bestia
Que también devora.

Mountain climbing
backpacks
fat with stacks of literature & stuff,
Desperately grope for
loftier peaks of lore.

While cats cling to the ivy leaves (?)
make love & meow
erecting in the process
towers not quite so ivory.

Y el cucaracho (noctural insect)
            por obscuros corredores
                        siempre va
cascariando y buscando
                  (en su soledad)

lo que un ayer no fue
                  y se pudo resisitir.

U of Washington/Seattle
1/'73

103

Homenaje al Pachuco
(Mirrored Reflections)

¡Ese Loco . . .
                    cúrate!
Dig on what/
        on what them dudes are saying,
                    VATO.
That you are (¡ja-ja, que lucas!):
        a non-goal oriented
                    alienated being,
                        sufriendo un "identity-crisis",
rejecting conventional modes & mores.
        ¡Me La Rayo!

Y wacha,
        dizque you sprang from EL CHUCO,
Boogie'd into LOS
                    & found
                            the battleground
for US Naval wars;
        y es acá.
Órale, simón que sí.

But check THIZ / quiz OUT
        en l'escuelín:
                PACHUCO MYTHOLOGY   — Room 1
                PACHUCO LANGUAGE
                    Caló: Patois, Argot, or Jargon   — Room 2
                THE PACHUCHO AS A POP-HERO — Room 3
                PACHUCO: MISCREANT OR
                                SOCIAL DEVIANT   — Room 4
                PACHUCHO PHILOSOPHY   — Room 5
                THE PACHUCO AS PACHUCO   — Room 6

Isn't that far out?
         ¿Y la extensión/evolución?
                 ¿A León?
As if to say
         (besides that your tramos were perhaps
                 from Pachuca — en el terre — where
                         campesinos wear piyama drapes)
that carnales: Pachucos/Vatos Locos/Low Riders/Yuvinales/
                 Midgets/Juniors/Chavalones/Veteranos/
                                                         Hipsters/
                 Conección/Kin'pin-Machín/
                 don't   still   fill
         las cárceles de Aztlán.
That brothers don't
         still walk the prison-yard
en FLORENCE/SANTA/FOLSOM/ & CAÑON
                 (¿y la federal?)
Que no piscan algoda
         (gimme some alagodone, MESKIN)
en la TEJANA
         aquel animal tan horroroso.

As if to say that
         RAZA Blood
                 does not continue flowing
on the GOD-DAMNED, gloomy streets
         of this Oppressive-racist,
                 Creative-Stifling
                         PINCHE SOCIEDAD!!!!

That CARNATION didn't fall in QUENTIN,
         CAMELLO no quedó tasajeado en el Rancho HARLEM
                                                         No. 1
         (or was it BLUE RIDGE Kamp?).

That MAMULA didn't drive
    bullet-riddled Buick
        into the heart of the barrio
    & died con cuete en mano.
Qu'el BOÑO de Watts
    isn't doing LIFE.
As if to add
    insult to injury,
one chump went on to say
    you died a-borning!!!
        ¿Qui'ubo?
Pero lo más sura was
    that in all their
        SOCIOLOGICAL
        ANTHROPOLOGICAL
        PSYCHOLOGICAL
        & HISTORICAL
heaps & piles of boguish bullshit,
    our sister—La Pachuca—of the
        equal sufrimientos;
aquella carnalita que también,
    who also bore the brunt
        de toda la carrilla;
remained in their textbooks
        ANONYMOUS.

So when you found
    his Mickey-Mouse world
        too A-bominable to accept,
you reject.

What did he expect?
Pero ahí se va,
            no sweat,
                    tú nomás juégala fría
& wait.
     Por tu resistencia perdurable
            someday
                    he will grow tired
                    & go away.
¿Cómo la ves tú, compa?
     If we negate these further realities,
            ¡se salen!
Y le peleamos la causa al gringo
     that we're Not ahistorical.
Yet no mention
     que por esta pinche vida vas
            SUFRIENDO.
Dibujos—TONANTZÍN Y HUITZILOPOCHTLI—grabados,
     tatuados en tu piel bronceada
            con las
                    Ardientes Agujas
de esta gacha sociedad;
                    que no sabe llorar
por niños hambrientos o migrantes sin trabajo.
     Much less give a damn, a good god-damn
            about
                    street-corner born,
                            forlorn fugitives
of the total jail
     Hail Pachuco!

                            Seattle, Washington
                            10 de febrero de 1973

Canto
(just for the hell of it)

Tú
 y
  Yo
   cucaracho . . .
parnas desde aquel entonces
      de
colchas calientitas   y
          veredas solitarias
con 'buelita Mane
      y tía Mage

Cuates desde los primeros años
      de abandono . . .
          nuestra huerfandad.

      "No tengo padre
      ni madre,
      ni un perrito
      que me ladre."

The first chingazos/
          cabronazos
Early slashes/
      gashes
from the piercing
      Knife
          of
          Life.

Escondidos/
      asustados
   en rincones de
      la cárcel del terror.

Después de largos (y amargos) años;
mountains de ladrio
      & rejas of steel
were pulverized/internalized/
       & CRYSTALLIZED
(con ayuda de la voz de rebelión).
    We brewed that batch
       de vino dulce
for brothers/sisters/gente
    (thirsty people)
      to partake.

Y ahora, ¿qué haces aquí?
      UUUUUUU - NIIIIII -
              versitario!
¿Qué chingaos haces aquí . . . ?
con todos estos Ph.D.'s
spouting polyglot abstractions
(those nowhere distractions)
which we cannot CONceptualize.

Con La Mujer
      de ayer
         que se dice ser
muy "sensitive."
Ms. Carrerista/ proud Feminista
to you . . . RoAcH.
      "No tengo madre
      ni padre,
      ni un perrito
      que me ladre."
(much less a La Fabulosa. . . bruto!)
El descuento, cucaracho, el descuento.
      ¡Se vale!

Besides,
        you know how
                to do it up
                        GOOD!
¿Tú dirás si destruyemos?
HOME
        is in the arms
cicatrizados/marcados/tatuados
        con los traques
                y los callos
Needle-marks
        INJECTED
                (not always by society)
but by one's own kind as well.

Y dice el cuento:
that the Aztec warrior
told an India fair (in Nahua dialect)
"though i must do battle,
adorn my spear with plumage bright
so that THEY know . . . and understand,
i acted out of Love."

Si pudieras volver
        a las jaulas horrorosas
                y avisarle a los demás
¿Qué les dirías?
        ¿Qué es ilusión
                purita diversión,
                        que no la agarren tan en serio?
¿Qué es puro pedo,
        that folks be living
                instead of giving?
That they be jiving
        a slick conniving,
                the righteous Jeff?

O simplemente,
    that
        the formula
did
  NOT
     work?

Y a según el cuento:
La India then replied
"Should you not return from battle,
it matters not the brilliance
of my Quetzal plumes,
nor the deadly keenness
of your spear. Only that
your cantos (for whatever reasons)
remain to sing of US
in terminology so unique."

         ¡CHAIN - ges!

Y los llantos que se oyen
      cada vez
que pasas por la mar
     ¿Qué pues?

Pero no demore
espejo/imagen/retrato/figura
camarada (salvación y destrucción)
Cucaracho of
         un/FEELINGS.
You/
    i know
        me/you
ev'thang gon' bees aw-right!

Y allí, donde
      El Guerrero cayó
          (refusing to turn back)
dejó grabado/con sangre/en la arena
for future pioneers & foragers,
creators de la Nueva Orden Social
to read 'n' heed 'n' carry on:

"¡Todos Está De Aquellas!"

              Seattle, Washington / 3/4/73

Extensions of an Evergoing Voyage

Viaje 'tras viaje
       conección sin herraje
Flashes! . . . of the Enchanted Lands
flashes de Nuevo Méjico . . .
       in the year of Resistencia
       in the year of no Piñón.
Finding/
       winding, wooded
ways.
Days spent with
       village viejitos
and young liberadores.
The chat with the gnat
the talk with the trees/
bees buzz by
       complementing/ enhancing
the rhythms & rhymes
of times when
       men/ women & nature
were one.
Canyon campfire poesía/
       alegría of cantos
with new Adelitas/
       rebeldes of now.

"The outcry of the North"
       heard once again
resounding through
       silent-sleeping/
pine-scented/ socially-seething/
       Montezuma wind.

(II)

Jersey, too . . .
          attempts to hide
               and chide
Portorican farmworkers kaptive
          on Atlantic Seacoast
                    slave (plantation) quarters . . .
                         now called labor kamps.
     Spirits ever high
     DEFY
the exploitation in the fields
     as songs are sung in solidarity;
"Yo Soy Chicano, Sí Señor/ Borinquen Querida, tierra de
                                        mi amor."

Soul-groceries provided/
               invited/him
                    poeta loco
(busy greasin' on Arroz-con-pollo
     y habichuelitas)
missing out on tasty pastelitos!

(III)

¿Qué chingaos tengo yo que ver
          con Liberty Bell
               when Hell
     is
     Black 'n' Brown Boricua babies
          burning/ gagging/ dying
               in the stinking squalor
of North Philly arrabal?

Through burned-out veins
      & arteries long collapsed
we view
      (hewn out of granite & buck$)
        huckter
            fucking people up
for GOOD.
The very heart of the MONSTRUO!!!

(IV)

"This is it, Maestas!"
      Heckle 'n' Jeckle
        dig
           big (ROTTEN) Apple.
Scraps of gente
      by the derelict thousands
        on 42nd St.
LOOK!
      with human hunger in their eyes.
The worm squirms
      through Gotham's
        nether worlds.
Graffiti
      People's Art
        on subways
           serious/graphical decor
for lack of canvases
      or breathing space
Refusing to face extinction.
in midnite sites of sights
      we walk 'n' talk
        down desolation avenues,
4 a.m. strolls
of people patrols
      in HarlemTown
where no BIRD blew for us,

& the color of your skin
still determines if you're IN . . .
even though you got
2 'ho's bartering
on the slave-block
Pockets (pollution) of Pigs
cast digs
on Blk. Liberation Ar-mee!
El Barrio
(Spanish Harlem)
apaga sus luces and puts itself to bed.
Meanwhile
En el Bronx al Sur:
war-torn, battle-scarred
ghetto prisons crumble
in devastating decay.
En el Bronx al Sur:
donde el traficante is the cop
& slum-bred dogs
(all lean 'n' hungry)
display/ portray
on protruding ribs
a righteous impression
of their oppression.
El Latin Palace Bar:
á go-go girls dance into oblivion
in color tones of earth.
(no nutmeg, bronze, canela,
choco/late, brown sugar tones)
but hues of EARTH!
Esa tierra
which was used & abused
long before that bubbling cauldron/
melting pot spewed
hot molten steel of greed
upon Mestizo seed.

El Toñito (del PSP)
      con hard-hat y toda la cosa
            (¡tan lindas contradictions!)
Says of mañana's march for Independence,
      "¡Esto no para aquí, Coño,
            tiene que cambiar!"
"Neruda just died!"
      cried Naomi
            (la viejita comunista).
"¡Lo mataron!", dije yo.
Como mataron a Lorca . . .
como mataron a Rigoberto . . .
the way they kill all poets.
      and if he died
of cancer . . . or a broken heart,
      i still maintain:
"¡La junta lo mató!"

          (V)

In Denver
      bombed-out (with real bombs!)
hulks of buildings stand
      defiantly as monuments to Luis Jr. Martinez
and other fallen warriors of our land.
      Y las niñas in their timeless trenzas
knowing the man's way
      choose to stay,
despite their proximity to war.
The Kourts of Kangaroo
      would send forevermore
            our soldiers to their doom
"Joe Gaitan must not die!"

Constantemente,
La Güerita (of the dual-soul)
nursed the ill, religiously,
con su té de canela y choco/late mejicano,
Then offered 7 daffodils
in return for a kiss
    "well-kissed"
a bandana (from tierras sagradas) for my Sun
Someday,
    perhaps,
we'll be exchanging guns.

Sept. '73/Sept. '74
2 cross-country
    (Seattle-to-New York
    and-in-between)
    trips.

A'nque la Jaula Sea on Campus No Deja de Ser Prisión

The Prof.
    (entre rejas
ethnic/
    ly
-terarias)
    DIScourses with alumnUS
the lesson for today.
Shit!
    instead of reading Po' Show
i dug B.B. King all night.
There was a need to drown/
    not hear the furtive footsteps
of nightwatch prison-guard
    making the rounds
outside my dormitory (celda nueva)
    Room 710. . . Commodore-Duchess
hotel/ motel . . . hell, JAIL!
La mente (pinta-accustomed) pregnant
    with
        ideas/stories/vidas
(of talonas & Nencía)
    screaming to be born!

We interpret (?)
    (Altruistically, of course)
el comienzo de NUESTROS barrios
while the cucaracho (lejos de SU Barrio)
    grapples/wrestles
(close to losing)
    with devastating demons out of the past
lives
    wondering if pachuco-poets of El Paso
dealt with those demonios too,
    as we & Malaquías Sr. did, indeed.

O' Malaquías of 1930s penitenciaría Leavenworth,
where decades later poets become inheritors
            of demon-dens (ánimas penando?) left to haunt
                nueva generación of colegas/
who in turn become colegas of artistpoetas
3rd party removed . . . on whom i'll now unload
            my bags all full of ogros.

Después the pinto prosodist begins to scat 'n' chant
            (daydreamin' y tripiando un escant'):
"Oooh . . . if i could stride with keen toe soles . . .
                keen toe soles . . . keen toe soles . . .
            if i could stride with keen toe soles,
            what then would i become?"
Part of a stable of 'ho's, perhaps?
Güisa que guisa gusanos grammarian, ¿quizás?
        ¡Záz!
scoo-didly-a-bop/ pop went the poesy.
Chew-cho . . . O' . . . Anty Chew-cho?
Class disMISSED.

Seattle / 1973

"Pssst! ¡Ese Joe, te Habla el Roy!"

i still recall
that day in SACRA/mento Fall
while not being poetas.
Simply (simple) gente/parentela
familia (toda la ralea)
todos jalea!
tirando birthday party pi-ki-nik
(pa'l General, ¡compa!)
con todo el escuadrón.
Pilotos de aroplas rotos
(todos motos, of course!)
pero con chingos de sal y pimienta.
TÚ . . . yo,
Tus Hijos, who were MY Hijos,
for the moment.
¿Recuerdas, José?

This was no time to rap of demons
(whom i had wanted you to meet).
However demons lurked (as demons usually lurk)
y con la pluma ardiente
(lonely weapon)
fiercely fight the furtive monsters,
struggling with the serpents of surrender
constant battle with the beasts who would devour us,
para matar once and for all
esos demonios desgraciados
with humbleness/poesía/& love.

¿Recuerdas, José . . . before
nights in the San Jo
of our chavalada vagabond?
(Visions de ciruela y chavacano.)
You read my Malaquías poem
& saw the world from dungeon/cuevas/pit

through jefe & colega (mutilated eyes).
¡Ha de habar sido un viejo muy maciso!
Lágrimas de Lucy (jefita . . . puro oro molido)
iluminaron livingroom floor,
bed.
¡Y a tirar carpeta se ha dicho!
We had established a base.
(Chale, pero no pa' usar de landing strip, ese . . . unless . . .
tripping-out on Villa's waaaaayy-ouuuuut astro-dream!)
cinchando el breakfast dominó.
¿'Tá darío el vato, no?
Tears of nostalgia i remember.
Healthy flow of laughter
conversations with profetas/bards/
MADmen/ madWOMEN
of this time/space universe.
& as the Western night reached out/
pulled down the shade
glimpses caught
in the glistening of a Guatemalan Sun
scurrying creatures we saw
attempting assault on basket/
san'wiches of salvation . . . for REALS!
feels good to be reLEASED.
Eased of psychic pain
Maintaining, NO Jive!
Smooth Swan dives/
jack-knives off the cliff
as
riffs of rhythm
cantan
clavados del puente
Viejo
(¡me hago y no me arrugo!)
we count candles en el qué-que,
while the huercos smiling/
laugh us into one more year

fearing no weirdos nor the river's depth.
Complete communion con la comunidad
edad of old/new generaciones
canciones coaxing al anochecer.
Glowing embers
smouldered
slowing the setting
of a soothing
Sexto Sol.
Remember?

                              Seattle 1974

Because I Should
(Un Breve Escape a Las Tierras Indias)

for Elda

Airborne
    once more
        (¡traes jeverín, Chuy!)
        the journey home
            BEGINS
A re-emplazer
        familias rendidas/
    devastated por propias manos
    (aside from the real problem).

¿Qué se dice
        en momentos tensos y astringentes?
Halo? . . . ¿Aquí estoy?
        Perhaps
a simple "¡Qui'ubo, Loco!"
        would suffice,
        if only . . .

Coming into Portland,
    René-dominated thoughts
        impose their density
as radiant eyes bespeak:
    "Somos hijos de AQUELLOS hijos."
Entonces,
    la reclamación should be made,
              ¿que no?
Stand for what is,
        or fall back on what was?
Poem to my jefe
        comes to haunt child's mind

forcing the utterance:
                    "we became what we became,"
                    deep into tender psyche;
                    as with a jagged blade.
But that is
        NOT
            el sobre-todo.
La Plebe
        enters jointly/
            communally
                into phase siguiente.
Why play a role
            (con las patas chorreadas)
                That's jive & unessential?
Don't compromise
        your stance
            POLITICAL
y trata de comunicarte así.
¿Sabes que BRANIFF serves scab lettuce?
    y aquí en el aire
también hay para-bailes.
            Yeah, i know Boss-Lady,
WE . . . gots to . . . DEAL . . . with . . . IT.
    (¡Pero está cabrón!)

Bajo el cielo de Aztlán,
        will it make a difference?
Raza Linda, ya volví
        me fue muy bien por allá
surge otra dimensión
        ya no soy de acá.
There's tristeza/ there is joy
        pero ya todo acabó . . .
hay que empezar otra vez,
        life has just begun
Excited apprehension mounts . . .
        will their faces be the same?

Will long hair make all the difference?
    Alienation will set in?
But there's a message to impart!
        i've changed, you-all!
(or have i?)

Te digo, Kiñena, que no es un pedo . . . ¡son varios!

Excited apprehension mounts . . .
        as this ave de aluminio
punctures passing thunderclouds
        and catches up with
a 95 degree,
            coming-into-Austin/Tejas/Aztlán-
                    verano night
                    of
                        unexpected
                        a - n - s - I - E - D - A - D!!!

                                Seattle/Portland/Austin
                                26 y 27 de Mayo del 1973

Austin, Tejas: Revisited

Y que pa' pronto caí . . .
        back to the garden
donde se hicieron nurture
        las flores/hierbas
of my happy/lonely juventud.
        Faces & places . . .
traces of a long-gone past.
        Gente de la cual
brotaron poemas/exploding guns
        from within the WALL;
to sing & cry of our
        EXISTENCE!

Primera noche
        of mucho rollo with righteous
caring-for carnales y carnalas.
        Constant-rapid-rapping
with the barman: El mayor
        of THAT familia,
recordando hermanos fallecidos
        (IN MEMORIAM: RICHE).

Night of alegres
        risas/carcajadas
& tristes
        balazos/filorazos
in that evanescent época
        of El Oriental Lounge.

¡En Chinnnn-ga!
     racing through San Marcos
(flashback to Seattle)
     of Chuy-Flaco
y del Tino . . . student days,
     con rumbo al Valle Trágico/
no longer Mágico.
     Ratos bittersweet
con la serene Serrana
     (who never had a poem unto herself),
reminiscing de las piscas
     remendando costales/
componiendo garsoles.
     Spirit of Jacinto Treviño
zumba/tumba
     neo-colonialismo-Tejas style.
Reunión calurosa
     con Chacón y Ramón
(tú nos hiciste los puños, penitencia Leavenworth)
     conceptos de lucha volando/
on the wing
     as if progressive palomas
          (rojas)
de Liberación.
Tercer noche de bailes . . .
     (recuerdos del USO y Skyline Club)
tirando suela to the
     Central Tejas/Tex-Mex/
down-home/Contemporary Raza/
     Chicano Sounds!
"Ya baila tu primo, María."

Tardes primaverales
            of maternal conflict
barriers/defenses.
            El no aceptar is
as painful as to accept.
            Te saludo a mi manera
and all that you can say is
            que te ofende mi greñota larga.
We bee's talkin' 'bout change, Mother!
            SOCIAL/REVOUTIONARY CHANGE.
Cambio de estructuras decadentes
            of tradition/culture/& valores.
¡Cambio! ¡Cambio! ¡Cambio por total!

                                    June '73

Canción de La Bahía

In San Francisco Town   i
              b   b
          u   a
    City of calles de s   j
                   a

(neighborhood of endless hills?)
    once stomping-grounds
        of BEAT poetas/
            other poetic renaissance.

Now,
    home which breeds,
from struggling seeds,
    Mad / Bad / in-SANE
              POETAS
who
    Dee-Fine
        lo nuestro
(¡Ábranle, que aquí viene la Raza!)

Roberto canta . . .
Murguía canta . . .
    y
      Dorinda
        se da topes
           con los meros caponeros;
then we all cry
        because we feel the devastation
          of the streets on
            lost Latino younglings
future músicos/ pintores/ y poetas
  (soldiers all)
    who will never be.

Curbing body hunger
            intravenously
("IN THE MIDDLE OF THE MISSION")
      they
            pump 'n' squirt
            narco-Nixon-Ponzoña
become criminal statistics/
      víctimas del opresor;
            en la 24 y la Misión
            (in the heart of selva-urbana).

¡Ay San Francisco,
      que tanto has dado
      y tanto has quitado!
We'll not jump off your Golden Gate
                              ¡Chale!

En Huehuetitlán
      the place where artesanos gather
            to do the things that artesanos do . . .
            allí mi corazón está.

Y en otras partes, too,
      my heart reposes / languishes . . .
            donde (at least for a while)
brillaron 2 de los 7 soles.
Tardeada Chicana
      laced with
            intricate musical tapestries—
y El Camarón
      (in mescalina-madness)
brings back to mind
      the terrifying days
            of man-child prisoners

(tecatos tejanos)
     'tras de las rejas
        of that west coast dungeon.
          S O L E D A D .

Street-Corner Dude
    makes jazz-latino sounds
        as magic fluegelhorn
creates sad smiles
    in the corners
        de ciertos ojos.
Me curo/ hago contemplate
    the statuesque paisana
        in green/white LOVEliness
and feel the soft & subtle
    gentle caricias,
while 10 -year old congaista
    generates the necessary heat.
("¡Qué toque Gasca!. . . ¡Gasca is Raza!. . . ¡Póngale,
                          Carnal!")
    "Oye como va" . . . "Suavecito, um-hum" . . .
                            "Guajira".
Parranda larga
      as usual
          y rezos hacia el Holy Smoke.
Mientras, marine-life panorama
    hizo surround & complement
        strong hermosura/ countenance
          of
            la Misteriosa.

O' fleas . . .
    you lucky, lucky fleas
        (qué casualidad that only in THAT rincón
                   hicieron nido!).

Intense poetic vibes
    as scribes meander down LatinoAmérica avenues
        la dulce música de voces ringing
"¿Oye coño, pero qué tú trae?"
Aromas/ cuchifritos
    pupusas
        picadillo
            y las frutas
                de aquel pueblo

oprimido—
        utopia of the mind—
                Managua.
MESSAGE TO THE OUTER WORLD:
    (as brother Pietri ran it down)
        AQUÍ
    se habla
        español-Chicano-pocho-slang-hip-caló
            y pa' cabarla de chingar,
                we also spik eengleesh, también!

Dali-esque surreal scene
    en mueblería del barrio
        John Dean (24 of him)
            in dying color
snitches
    for the folks in TV land.
        He rats and tells
            on Lottie/ Dottie/
                & everybody.

watergate has sprung a leak
                    come take a peek
                            then we shall seek
to build/
    create
        a new society
                from the shambles
of this decadent—llena de podredumbre—assassin of pueblos
BABYLON . . . ameriKKKa!

                                el 29 de junio del 1973
                                Seattle, Washington

134

Sola Se Masturba

Alone . . .
    she masturbates
Hypnotically
    she flails into
        Orgasmic Dimensiones
gnawing/clawing
    at shadows of past (no) lovers/
        shovers
    reeling
      on
      peeling,
broken
    mirror
      of
        the
        SOUL.

En su erotic imaginación
    there seems no need for
    sexual/visual aids.
Nada más que remnants
    (ebritas del ayer)
        of days & nights sin lágrimas,
frustrated fantasies,
    un Dedo,
& much mechanical manipulation.

She
>   COMES!
>   >   >   >   Violently/Maniacally/Obsessively
entranced
>   she grasps/
>   >   embraces lover-finger
while torrential tears
>   of Passion
>   >   play a dirge
drowning could've (and would've) been rucos
>   then
>   >   fall
>   >   >   like wasted seed
(absorbed)
>   into a musty book.
i feel for her
>   as
>   >   alone
>   >   >   she
>   >   >   >   masturbates.

>   >   >   >   14 de agosto de 1973
>   >   >   >   Seattle, Washington

Poetica: Notes from New York

          Miguel/ Miguelín
          Piñero/ Algarín
          remain within
          el cora
                  (poetic)
                  de Aztlán.

Likewise
      (también, coño)
Lucky CienFuegos
Lower Eastside
          SPAAAAAAACE . . . MAAAAAN!
Boricua namesake
      del Cuban Camilo
(compañero of Ché
          & Fidel),
con su
      electrifyin' afro
(universo tropical)
statically sprouting
          chispas/ poemas
                  & sparks——
stark canciones of Life,
stone cold
          6th Street
Nuyorican Life
          rife w/ niños
puchando tabaco
(in bags y rolao)
          & hypos
volteaos al revez.

El Poeta Chingón
Don Jorge Brandon
        (with his talking coconut)
w/ all of his obra
        fajada en el cinturón.
"SHORT EYES"
        a bad
                po'to rican pinto's play
just hit Lincoln Center
just hit Tin Pan Alley in the face
        & Mikey still very much himself
keeps spending his advancing checks
        in curbing people's hunger
                (coca/hero . . . ina
                        hero sandwiches/ fritangas)
on sweltering insomniac
        Manhattan ghetto streets.

                                lower east side, nyc
                                octubre de 1973

A Touch of Life

for Tina Maestas

The children sang,
        their voices rang
like crystal (freedom) bells
        within my weary soul.
    Scrambled emotions/
        nice notions of
            the night before
& guilt for all
        the unwritten
            revolutionary papers.
Third World toddlers play
"ring-around-the-rosey . . ."
in an almost forgotten
        playground of my mind,
while Chile is no longer news
        and Middle-East madness
                increases.

¡ALLENDE!
        con una lágrima llorona . . .
te envuelvo en la nostalgia/
        las memorias
            of my
        Juventud,
(y te recuerdo en el olvido).
                ¡ALLENDE!

The children sang
        a song not to be
                silenced by oppression.
A song not to be stilled
        by lords of war
i heard the children
        sing today
& recognized the future
        of the world.

(i heard the children
        sing today . . .)

                25 de diciembre de 1973
                Seattle

Flowerless Winter

Bidding
      for
         YOU
in forbidden
      corners of par/ tee
i finally settled
      for taking
         your dimpled-smiles
            to bed with me.

Days later
      you came by
         to pick them up;
i offered you a steaming cup
      of hot-spiced wine
         fine feelings
            & recipe sans ice.

           In
         not-too
klassy kitchenette
      we giggle,
         save on wine. . .
half-full glasses for the guests.
Yr. tiny, miniature
      & unrestricted
         Breasts
           (quite free)
keeping making eyes at me.

Each time you leave
and you MUST leave
poetic essence grieves
cringing soul from searing pain
of promises to come again.
        Y VOLVERÉ
                the last selection
you play
        before tearing away
                equipped with
                        2 teardrops from a lacerated heart
                        1 ready-to-be-born (gestating) poem
                        & my favorite tattoo, reproduced.
i hate to see you go.
My reclusive room
        receives you well
                these days.
i make love
        to you
(upon surrealistic pillow)
        on nights
                when one side
of my pull-down,
                Murphy bed
                        stays cold.

Dreary dawn
of unplanned papers
& unexpected capers
        engaged in serious quest
as liberators.

And then we frowned
        at obviously oppressive brand
            your wedding band
which equalled,
      you said,
          the handcuff
              on
                 my
                    wrist.

                    Seattle
                    January 1974

It's Been Two Years Now

since i left that
isolation cell
in Marion Prison . . .
From that time on
(my heart always/
ever/ overaccelerating)
i have:
become as one
with struggles of
world social movements,
done 392 poetry readings
(most without pay),
written of my myriad lives
still have no transportation
(other than my feet,
and that beats a blank),
met viejito socialist poets
(who can be more interesting
than cultural nationalist poets),
held no steady job,
loitered 'round the fringes/
annoying alleyways of academe
(knowing quite well
the danger there),
fallen in love 8 times,
fallen out of love 8 times,
and still i love and Love
and LOVE again,
been in anthologies
(four to be exact)
with more (2) to come,
and i become a 1
(correction: 2) poem
poet,

While quite obscured
lines carved on tree trunks
verses spray painted in halls
songs scratched on walls of
countless concrete caves
(THOSE 18 YEARS OF HELL!!!)
go undetected.
i have also:
consulted/
insulted
pedagogue professors
who profess to know the ALL.
been guilty of facilitating
theses and dissertations
with searing shreds
of ME
resulting in someone's degree
as i falter and flounder
pondering upon the fate
of the freshman at forty.

November 1974
Seattle

Capítulo Dos

Here
    come
        those
            BLOOZ
                again.

The gloomy face
    of this ciudad
        recreates los mismos
            gestos
                one more once.

But
    joyful spirits
        of last quarter's
            estudiantes
                crack the silent drear

of
    empty/
        estéril/
            Lander Hall

&
    Epi's marijuana
        giggles
            laugh away
                my blues.

Después,
    beneath moist/
        misty blankets
            the sleeping city
            yawns.

Dawnsongs
        i sing
          to
   mystic maidens
         of
unrelenting rains,
sad eyes (that only make me sadder),
the struggle (somewhat) defined,
Love

and
   the
anticipation
     of
       Spring.

Late '74
Seattle

Muse-Moving Mountain

II

Cold
    &
        indifferent
    Mt. Rainier;
you stand aloof,
    as down
        los pinches callejones . . .
brothers - sisters
    stumble/ fumble
        on obstacles/ barreras
of colonized
    Austion.
They swim in
    murky depths of
        burnt-out silverware
and die
    a thousand
        junkie-deaths.

III

i'd love to
    screw you, MAMA
        Mt. Rainier;
if only
    i could find
        your hole
to prick my stick
    of dynamite
        in YOU.

VI

Even tho'
　　　you ice/ ly
nice/ ly!
　　　(momentarily)
soothe my soul
　　　i cannot,
Mt. Rainier,
　　　forget we're
in a time of war
　　　and poets
must not rest
　　　too long.

VII

Clouds
　　　del amanecer
drip/ slip
　　'n' slide
　　　　down your erotic side
Hide and seeking games
　　you play
on the day when
　　　"Li'l Orange"
is in town.

1975
Seattle

IX

¡Chingao!
     Mt. Rainier,
you bum-
          kick me
at times.
TÚ,
que fascinas
     y capturas poetas/
aviadores locos.
Cocos of
     SacraCozmikArtistas
you fill with intoxicating
     ilusiones
and not even your
     calzones
did you show
     that
          day.

'74 - '75
Seattle

El artista más revolucionario sería aquel que estuviera dispuesto a
sacrificar hasta su propia vocación artística por la revolución.

—Nicolás Guillén

¡Nicolás!
negro canoso
you are old & wise
y yo tan joven
me muero, menos que un poeta
por la decadencia de mi país.

¡Nicolás!
i hear tambores beating
as i read your poems que expresan
las raíces of your negritud.
African rhythms tend to blend
con Latin blood to flood
Humanity
with revolutionary love.

Bajo Cubano skies
those yanqui-fabricated lies
will penetrate our social state
(of mind!)
no more.

Before my generation's blooming
as red roses
antes que iluminaran scarlet stars
creímos las mentiras del tirano
amerikano/ cara de marrano
breeder 'n' feeder of gusano nests.

Spring '75
Cuba

Beneath
  the ripening
Cuban, Springtime
  Mango trees —
Moist leaves
  fell
on
   the
  warm
          humid
             EARTH

in
   sweetened
          April
             EX-TASI!!

                              Guayabal
                              3/29/75

```
Palm trees
        appear
                piercing
crimson
        Oriente sun
which is
        (socialistically)
        Shared
                by
                        US.
```

```
                Santiago de Cuba
                4/10/75
```

May Day, Plaza de la Revolución, La Habana, '77.

Nightmare Number 13

Sueños fantasmas/
Fantasmas en sueños
   que se hacen dueños
de mi mendiga mente . . .
   mientras gente querida
se volca en volcanes
   (huracanes sexuales)
eruptando iguales
   que los horrores
(estadounidenses)
   dolores del alma
que en esta tierra
   de la palma
no dan calma
   hasta que haya pasado
la hora
     de
      la aurora

y
  El Sol
    picando los ojos
      (rojos) . . .
trae la salvación.

campamento julio antonio mella
guayabal, la habana, cuba
5/10/75

154

Unity Vision

(1st Chant)

Brief / respiteful
　　　precious (in the movement) cruise
　　　　　down desolate
1st & Spokane streets
　　　EVOKES
smoke-signals of past
　　　Seattle Springtime struggles /
　　　　　Sad Summer
　　　　　　　of Native tragedies /
　　　　　　　　　& Dallas Chicanito deaths.
From empty (wasting) warehouse rows
　　　a fleeting, darting, silent
　　　　　(momentary)
　　　　　　　SONG FOR SANTOS . . .
　　　　　　　. . . BLUES FOR WOUNDED KNEE.
The haunting humming of an Autumn wind
　　　decries historical lies /
　　　　　atrocious repetitions of blood.
The Trail
　　　(almost to no avail)
　　　　　of Broken Treaties,
resulting in more broken promises
　　　　　　　and rights
　　　　　　　and minds
　　　　　　　and souls
　　　　　　　and laws . . .
those flaws from the claws
　　　of a predator society
　　　　　seeking satiation
inside indigenous heart of earth.

Birth-rights bombarded /
        discarded life of
                innocent lamb-child
                SANTOS.
Warrior Drums
        (that speak of hope)
are sounding/
        pounding out
an angry call-to-arms.
Staccatoing
        super-sophisticated
weaponry of war
        implodes/ EXPLODES!
and Pedro Bissonette
        lies dead.
Peace-loving/ war-hating Bissonette
        BISON
                (human replica)
slaughtered
        in the Indian People's fight.
While
        Armored Personnel Carriers
                (murdering mammoths)
draw the line of demarcation
        the nation of the Sioux
                begins (again) to rise.
Wise South Dakota
        medicine man
smokes the pipe of peace
        & fans the fires of
                self-determination
Lakota people seeking liberation
        demanding to be free.

                                        August '75

156

Leonard Peltier trial, Milwaukee, January '78. Foto: La Guardia.

Forest/Desert Vision

(3rd Chant)

Far
       from northwestern
firs & forests,
away
       from mountain peaks
of snow which now glow
in the distance;
past
       vast populations
of western redlands/
ancient, ancestral sequoias,
is the Isle of Alcatraz
       where some of it
              (without a doubt)
                     began.
San Francisco
       where we learn
              that Sandino
is very much alive!
The Gypsy Woman also lives/
       engages catclysmic conversations/
promising to remember the warriors
       in her leaves of tea.
Freeway (new way?)
       bad way travel to L.A.
Monterrey Peninsula
       natural
mural panorama
       as
Salinas Valley
       stoically

lives down
steinbeck (reactionary) romanticism
of
still/ real
lettuce-picking campesino
& mission indio
stark realities.
And
SOLEDAD
mad-mutant monster
(robber of youth-full years
where tears & fears
gave way to
Piscean passion in
poetic & political eruptions)
hunkers hungering & sleepy yet
subsisting on
convicted cadavers
of the classless set.
As crop-dusting plane/
bane of all who till the soil
spoils (almost) clouding
positive sign
of high-flying Eagle
nearing (knowing we can't afford to stop)
Redwind
&
Semu's Camp.
3 times
the Eagle has appeared
(first . . . in Oregon, after the Portland
rally/march . . . documented as a good
symbol by traditional octogenarian
Granny Hillaire
of lush Suquamish lands.)
The third time was in Tejas
after spirit session

with Andres,
Aztec conchero dancer/
          Brujo of the arts
               who
(aware of the warmongers)
          also said
"things will be right in the valley of the roots."
This time (the 2nd one around)
          it soars over
meadow filled
Murrieta land
and San Miguel
of infamous
1800s indio
iron (fire) brandings.

After the Eagle
          came Semu.
Instantaneous thoughts
          of Southwestern sand paintings
and the Red Sister of the North
          who carves out her/our lives
in totemistic miniatures.
SEMU
          masterful merger
of blossoming human being
          communions.
SEMU
          grandfather of
                    EL TECOLOTL
                    DE
                    TESUQUE PUEBLO
                    C/S

SEMU
    who bid us to
"go South, for all is well,
        and it is safe to journey."
Downtown L.A.
    polluted parcel of earth
where buffalos (both red and brown)
        no longer roam,
banished/ practically vanished
        genocidal extinction
            from their home.

                    September '75
                    on the trail

Love / War
(a metamorphosis of sorts)

A
Hazy/ Lazy
(half-hidden)
Harvest Moon
Hung low/
Glowing on
two
(new) lovers
Slightly obscure
October Moon/
chameleon moon
of changing seasons
entices lovers
to exchange warm smiles/
tenderly touch hands

gripping each other firmly . . .
A
   long,
      last,
FINAL KISS
to ease the (burning)
          yearning
before turning
(in accordance with the struggle)
      into
flaming arrow
    &
obsidian axe.

        berkeley / s.f.
        oct. '75

Survival Song

In

fur-lined fas/cination
        petite-sized
fleeting fox
        (summer camper!)
scampers across
        criss-cross
S
  P
 I
R
  A
    Ling road
  Leading down to
  Grandma George's Beach.

Reaching out to
        meet 'n' greet
(by touching with the eyes)
this instant flash of
        fiery red-pelt radiance/
emanating natural
        NATIVE
           (magic!),
somehow makes
        Clam Digging
           easier
(for Indians)
        on this day.

        Suquamish Reservation
        Washington
        11/25/77

Prayer for a Newborn

for Ha'kwa'stobsh

Raccoon,
        spooning through
week's long garbage
on cabin front porch,
brings on good feelings.

    Blue Jay's breakfast
            on frybread/ by kitchen-sink window
——today's portion of meal——
            honoring our dead,
    and flying smiles
    and soaring soul
         heed heartsong
of elders and all:
"For those generations gone before us . . .
for the generations yet unborn."

    Inside
Mind/heart/soul
Eagle wings/
    fluttering feathers
Medicine man fans
    auras in good faith.

    Some die, so others live
that's how it gots to be.
All of us must struggle
so that someone may be free.

Because it's good to be alive
we ask all of the grampas
to walk 'n' talk with you . . .
we welcome you,
Red Cedar Man.
Hau!

jackie venable
dead in a prison cell
of toxic poisoning
sniffing too much gasoline.
snuffed his guitar
because he was lonely & sad
(teardrops dripping from his heart)
because he was Black
because his wife was White
because his child was Black 'n' White
in a world not right.
because he'd rather play jazz than rock 'n' roll.
because he was forced to play rock 'n' roll instead of jazz.
because of a genius which sought more
finding nothing/ winding up with less.
because he was weak,
because he was human . . .
his guitar never played again.

San Francisco
4/78

166

Cantiquitos

pa' 2 combatientes
beto y anuar

1

Sunday Morning
Church Campanas
Suenan
Mission Mamaces
Señoras Pray
SAN / DINO!
Prepare Protesta
Seriamente Supportive
Pueblo Peleando
¡Nicaragua!   2

Tempranito Sunrising
Mission Ritmos
Community Cantando
Survival Sonidos
Nocturnal Pueblo
Barrio Bailando
Daytime Gente
Latins Luchando
3   Humitos of Home.

Alive
Mission
Nicaragua Well
Sandino Lives
San Francisco
Streets Shout
Self-Determination.

4

Comunicado:
Nora Compañera
Personal Carácter
Militant Disciplina
Consciente
Obligations Compromisos
Revolucionarios
Northern Front
Pueblo Mujeres
Sister Inspiración
Activamente Participate
Proceso Worldwide
Insurrection Popular
Dictatorship Derrota
5   ¡Liberación!

Indigenous Machetes
Monimbó
Upraised Corajes
Castoff Colonialismo
Northwest Indios
Alegres Relations
Sonriendo Struggle
Gigs Fishing
Saludando Spears
Solidaridad.   6

Facing Somoza
Struggling Sandinistas
Learning Liberación
Nicaragua Free!

San Francisco
4/2/78

Barrio La Misión, '79. Foto: Kathy Apodaca.

Sacrasensación with Flying Colors

con cariño y respeto
a las compañeras y
compañeros del RCAF

(I)

After painful
    (como siempre)
San Francisco
    chavalo/ father
jefito/ son
    44th celebración (?)
& drive a san
Mateo makes solo flight,
    destination: Sacra
"meant to be here earlier, ese."

En chinga,
    en chivito prestao
("'56 & stock, bro.")
    salsacuba
spirit of vietnam.
    Calling forth
Sioux shaman
    spiritual man
fanning eagle feather
    messages/ words
como decir/ explain
    NECESIDAD
of building
    Raza/ Indian
SOLIDARIDAD.

Dejándome ver
just what's my deber
        i see
progressive semillas
        GEE! NAH!
seeds sprouted
        out of poetic
pasiones (once) unencumbered,
EXPLODING BOUQUETS!
        MARIPOSAS TATTOOED IN RED!
ARCOIRIS DANZA!
        SOARING COLORES DE FIESTA!
(wings well-earned)

        HE/ SHE
defensores indígenas
        do
symbolic security
        for
Abuelo of Dancing
        (prancing)
waters/
spread green mantillas
for mamá Tierra
        offering
mazorcas de maíz
        for
tata Sol/
        singing flores of love
pa' future generaciones/
        canciones
showers of flowers
        for the
nietecitos/ nietecitas
        of the
SUN.

Red-crested woodpecker/
blue jay from Cedar Woman
        Sacred Salmon lands
(one for each eye)
        wink at
quetzal/ paisano plumage
        recognizing still
ceremonies semejantes.

        Mientras Indias from other
Sands of Time
        saquean
klan plan kar-terr/
        Tecato TRIPtych
becomes "for reals"
        as long ago
holoGRAMS de Heroína
poisonous propina
enfermedad of our esquinas/
espinas in the lives of
        nuestros YOUth,
aparecen even aquí.
Because of that
¡Y más!
Venas once llenas de veneno
        hoy full of
Indígena/ Raza
        rabia/ rage
paciencia/ love
        & Resistencia.

Fables/
    Mad Monk Meanderings
monquean con seriesona
    poetic melona
causing ojos
    long having forgotten to laugh
to crack springtime sonrisas
    (¡brisas!)
on corners of EYE
    Street, instead of tea/
¡Te sales, vatito!
  tho' un poquito
    there-a-pew-tick!
i must admit
    quickly realizing
solución/ salvación
    essence of cure
within low-cure
    lo-CURA, enabling
viejitos/ viejotes
    cósmicos y locotes
juntos con Lacotahs
    INDIOS
a hacer
    l'UNIDAD.

Talkin' 'bout
	U-knee-tea
of
DedoGordo/ Águila Negra
	pioneering pilot
future forgers of
	The Way
and
	Pachuco Poetas
crudely compuestos
	of
  broken botellas de bironga
haunting horrors of heroin
a sense of struggle
	and LOVE.
Un "te quiero"
	CHICANINDIO
rebel yells y sombrerazos,
	CONCRETA(neta)mente speaking
a lo nach . . .

O' how la plática flowed
	days of no more glowing
ánforas de huayín
	Machín' rap of
ZOOT SUIT/ LOUIE/ HOMENAJE
	Pachucos Revisited.
"And Her Children (too) Shall Live"
	porque to give
aún que refín, mujer,
en fin, hemos de ver, is to receive/
	as weavings de solecitos
indigenous of 2 continentes
	calientitos
como un recuerdo
	we leave at your front door.

Después,
   under meditation árbol
(palo de moras)
   raza coras
hechan holy smoke rezos
a LIMOTZÍN
(fin del machín, sin rin!)
   días after
mind-blowing domingo
   en el parque:

as años atrás

also rifó
   then se quedó
casi en el olvido
   (aside del urban removal)
for fear que fuéramos
   a regresar/
fracasáramos all over again/
   too late for that.

Y allá
   en la olla de Montoya
five frijolitos/
   almost pilotitos
listos pa'l avión
   sirven (con amabilidad)
como
   comforting coffeebreaks en la Causa.

"Preparing for take-off, Vince!"
   Circles Sagrados complete,
"¡Y a volar se ha dicho!"

                    La Misión - San Francisco
                    3/23 - 29/78

Platicando en Memoria

a los herederos
de César Augusto Sandino

pa' Gato

¡Oye, Viejo!
       inspiración luchadora . . .
mal-encachado
       marina/navy nemesis
con tu gorro
       encasquetado hasta
las orejas . . .
       los yanquis oyeron llamadas
declaradas
       in
Nica-Tropi-Tempos
       of
guerrillero judged "insane."
       Humane
quisiste hacer tu país
       contra
asquerozas moscas toscas
       (mezcladas en mierda)
infecting la población.
       Compañero
              de las botas chuecas
carrilleras malforjadas
       desde que yo nací.
Digo, te hablo así,
       compay
porque en mi memoria
       siempre
quedas fijo
rostro serio
hombre humilde
libertador.   5/21/79 / Seattle

Song for Roland Kirk

(in a minor blues mode)

We all,
    (O' how weee!)
  LOVED
You
    (good)
mah god!
  RAHSAAN.

Shit!
    You spoke
in spirit tongues
    & things,
gave (some) folks
    irritating feelin'
wid yo' jokes
    of
Hurt & Pain
    Raining
      Jazz
        Tears
dispelling fears
  of
    being
      Sane.
You wuz close
  to
Something . . .
    Man!

Ballads/ Bullets
    Blown!
RAT-A-TAT-TATTING
    in the battle of
Struggling Saxophones
      (nose flute/ manzello & Stritch,
        instruments to befuddle the rich!)
SOUNDS
        that somehow
made it
    RIGHT
for
    US.

Blind Man
    (seeing all)
calling to heed
    1950s Austin
crowds of jazz
    leading
to good direction
helping those not blind
to
    SEE.

RAHSAAN/
    mah man,
it just feels
    SO GOOD!
to hear your sounds
    INFLATED TEAR
BRIGHT MOMENTS
    INTROSPECTION . . .
still wishing you
    (500-lb. Man)
was HERE.

Native Brothers/
        Sisters from the North,
they dug you too.
        i guess it was because
you
        talked to trees
Bees/ Birds
and things like that.

Small wonder
        (shit!)
the GREY world
        judged you
NUTS.
What else is new?

YOU
        (& me)
Knew
        (the bloooz)
it bee's
like dat
in sick society
gone
        MAD!!!

                                        Seattle
                                        1979

Because I Dared to Love

It's been a helluva' year
    DEAR/ly Beloved.
And as bittersweet
    Cocaine
dreamily drains
    Up
       n'
        D
          o
        w
           n
brown nasal pass/ age way
    swaying (stubbornly)
pensamientos
    tattooed by time
to that
    Suquamish Summer
day of rending pain.

It didn't rain
    that muted month,
remember love?

Roving raccoons' raid
        barely paid-for
groceries recently bought.
Fought for days on end
    bending the bonds
(fronds of boston fern)
    frown

as
    TIES
        (supposedly tempered)
by STRUGGLE & LOVE
    dissolve
        into
           LIES.
Now /
    somehow
nostalgic notions
    CON/jure
mixed emotions
    gladness
        sadness
only . . .
    for the lonely/
Ness is gone;
    Done for!
        Killed?

Still,
    around the corner
(como siempre)
there' a tempting/
    tantalizing/
teasing taste
    (of no escaping)

YOU.

                            Seattle
                            1979

NOTA SOBRE "LOS MONTOYA"—¿Why José? ¿Por qué Malaquías? Juntos (blood soul brothers) pero (Sacramento/ Oakland) no revueltos. Because shattered/smattered espejos de post (preMATURE, quizás) pachuco duelos/blues saltaron como reflejos de tiempos complejos sprouting from canvases (lonas rotas) torn por el viento del valle, murallas that somehow penetraron prison walls. También, porque pachuca portraits/ painted poems of nonpoetic pasado revelaron retras literartísticos. Signposts quedaron para siempre en el camino, immortalizing barrio landmarks . . . definiendo el sabor (saber) of our aesthetics.

Porque cartelones (rótulos for manifestaciones) depicting luchas of three continents merged enMASSe/ passing through prison poets' antiparras/ blinding bartolina barras notwithstanding. Because of Vietnam horrors that broadened visionscope of strugglers sequestered . . . good feelings for a future less insane. Because of tender moments shared in poems / palettes, pain/placeres del vivir. Compañeros (compañía) in the lonely, solitary acto de crear.

Porque es un honor to have these two progressive cultural worker/Artistas (both of whom have many times gone unacknowledged) colaborando/ compartiendo en conjunto conmigo en esta humilde creación. Por un spiritual affinity/por respeto/por amor. Por todo esto y mucho más.

r.r.s.
Feb. 14, 1980

2:|0|0|
3   5/09